# The 12-Week Anxiety Relief Workbook

## A Guided Workbook and Journal with Prompts to Calm Anxiety, Relieve Stress, and Practice Daily Self-Care

**ROMA SHARMA**

FIRST EDITION, SELF-PUBLISHED BY ROMA SHARMA
PRINTED IN INDIA

# This Journal Belongs to

..........................................

# Introduction

Welcome to a new chapter of your life. I am excited to share this journal with you. I am a certified counselor and trainer working in the field of emotional well-being since 2014. During my career, I have authored several books and developed courses that have positively influenced the lives of over 25,000 individuals worldwide.

Stress, tension, and anxiety have become common experiences for people in today's fast-paced world. Balancing work pressures, relationships, and other responsibilities can often be overwhelming. Achieving external success while feeling depleted internally due to stress is not a measure of success.

In the midst of tackling life's challenges and pursuing your greatest aspirations, it is important to establish a self-care system that can help you effectively contribute to your work and the well-being of your loved ones. This journal has been created to facilitate this objective. It is designed to help you overcome anxiety and nurture a sense of inner calm while taking on the challenges of daily life.

Through 12 weeks of consistent journaling, you will acquire specific techniques to understand and manage your anxiety. To fully harness the benefits of these methods, it is essential to allocate time for journaling each day. While this requires commitment, the long-term rewards will be significant. You will discover the ability to maintain a sense of calm and focus, even in the midst of difficult circumstances.

## COLOR THIS WITH GENTLE STROKES

# How to use this book

Hi,

Congratulations on taking the first step toward living an anxiety-free life.

This journal is divided into 12 sections—one for each week. Each week, we will learn new tools and techniques that will help you overcome anxiety and navigate through difficult days with ease.

Journal entry pages have been provided for each day of the 12-week program. Please take a few moments every day to write in them. At the end of each week, a weekly check-in sheet will help you reflect on the week that was. Additionally, monthly check-in sheets have been provided to reflect on your progress over the month.

Once you complete journaling for 12 weeks, assess the changes in yourself. You will notice that you are now able to remain peaceful in situations that previously made you anxious. Enjoy the process of becoming the calmest version of yourself.

*Sincerely,*

*Roma*

# Set a time & place aside

Set a place for writing your journal. This will help you get into the *journaling state of mind* faster.

Assign a time of the day to write your journal entry. Don't overthink your answers. Write down the first thing that comes to your mind, unedited. Also, please keep your journal in a private place.

WHAT WILL WRITING THIS
JOURNAL EVERY DAY GET YOU?

___________________________

___________________________

___________________________

___________________________

# The Root Cause of Anxiety

IF YOU CHANGE THE WAY
YOU LOOK AT THINGS, THE
THINGS YOU LOOK AT
CHANGE

— WAYNE DYER

# The Root Cause of Anxiety

Anxiety manifests as persistent worry, even in non-threatening situations. It typically arises from childhood experiences wherein a person faced overwhelming circumstances and may not have developed effective coping mechanisms.

This can lead to a learned helplessness mindset that often continues into adulthood. Over time, it becomes easier for the individual to slip into this state, even for matters they could formerly handle confidently.

Another factor that contributes to the development of anxiety in children is when they have a caregiver who models anxious behavior. If they observe their parents frequently displaying anxious tendencies, it becomes a familiar and normalized response to challenging situations.

This unconsciously shapes their coping mechanism. The child ends up adopting similar anxious behaviors as a way to navigate their own experiences without evaluating the benefits of doing so.

Whether we received a supportive and nurturing environment during our growing years or not, we can actively work on providing it for ourselves today.

Recognizing that our anxious behaviors are often rooted in situations we had no control over can help us be gentle with ourselves on this journey of change.

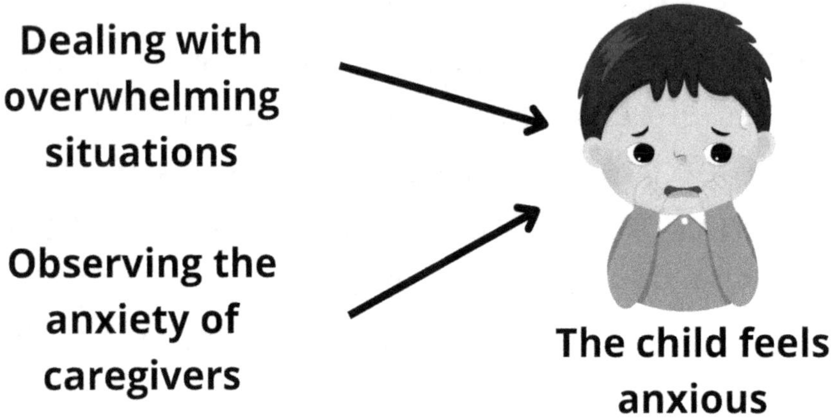

**Dealing with overwhelming situations**

**Observing the anxiety of caregivers**

**The child feels anxious**

Time travel

How did you manage your anxiety as a child?

______________________________________________

______________________________________________

______________________________________________

How did your caregivers, such as your parents, handle their own anxiety during your childhood?

______________________________________________

______________________________________________

______________________________________________

Do you notice any similarities between your coping mechanisms and those of your caregivers?

_______________________________________________

_______________________________________________

_______________________________________________

Is there a childhood coping mechanism that has persisted into adulthood that you would like to change?

_______________________________________________

_______________________________________________

_______________________________________________

What steps can you take to facilitate this change?

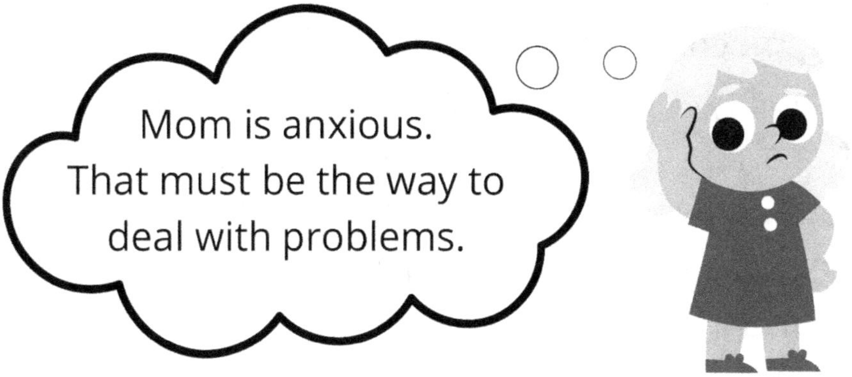

_______________________________________________

_______________________________________________

_______________________________________________

# Can we get rid of anxiety?

While it may not be possible to completely eliminate anxiety, we can discover ways to effectively manage it so that it does not dictate our lives. Being courageous is not the absence of fear. It is about being scared and doing what needs to be done anyway.

Every individual needs to develop their own methods to maintain inner calm amidst the chaos that life often brings. Your unique strategy will present itself to you once you experiment with the methods suggested in this book over the 12-week journaling program.

# Why face your anxiety?

Deciding to work on your fears requires courage. You might wonder if we really need to do this. Can't we just avoid the people who stress us out? Or remove the anxiety triggers from our life altogether?

Avoiding the people we fear isn't a long-term coping mechanism because it isolates us. We lose the ability to establish deep, meaningful relationships. We no longer believe that if something were to befall us, we will have the support we need. The thought of being alone in this world increases our anxiety.

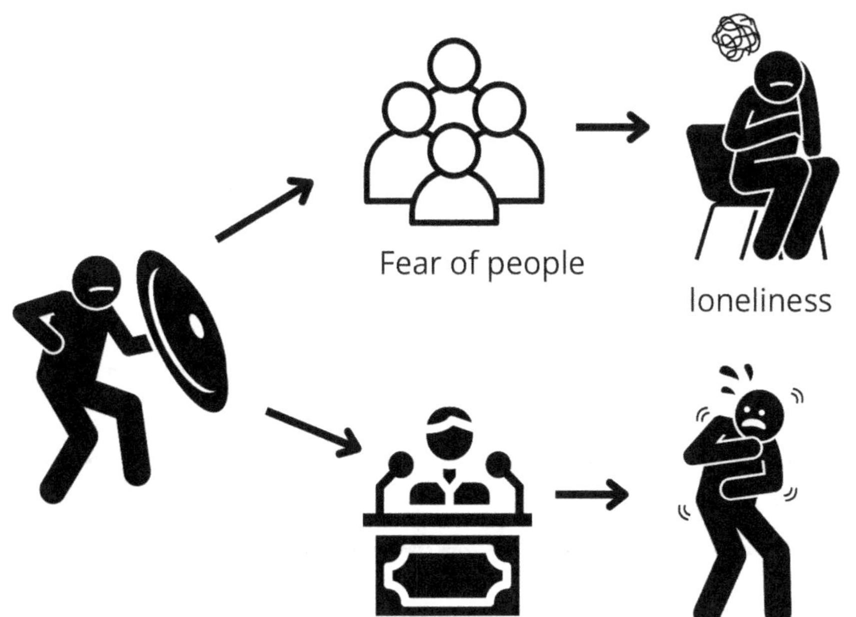


While it might be helpful to stay away from certain types of people or situations, it is necessary to ensure that it doesn't become a habitual way of dealing with anxiety triggers.

Prolonged avoidance can limit our growth. It perpetuates the cycle of anxiety by reinforcing the belief that these triggers are insurmountable threats, ultimately hindering our ability to develop effective coping mechanisms.

For instance, if I am always avoiding a certain type of person, I never learn the skill to deal with that type of person. Or if I am scared of public speaking and avoid giving presentations, I might miss out on great opportunities at work.

*Growth lies outside your comfort zone*

# Are you ready?

Do you believe it is possible to reduce your anxiety? On a scale of 1 to 10, how confident are you in your ability to do so?

_______________________________

_______________________________

_______________________________

If your confidence rating is below 5, is there something that can help you increase that number?

_______________________________

_______________________________

_______________________________

On a scale of 1 to 10, how strongly do you desire an anxiety-free life? If your rating is below 5, is there something that can help you increase that number?

_______________________________

_______________________________

_______________________________

# Name 4 things you love about your life

## Draw them below

# Monday

DATE:

TODAY I FELT

WHAT WAS ON MY MIND TODAY? HOW DID IT MAKE ME FEEL?

_______________________________________________

_______________________________________________

_______________________________________________

_______________________________________________

_______________________________________________

WHAT WENT WELL TODAY?

_________________________________

_________________________________

_________________________________

_________________________________

_________________________________

_________________________________

_________________________________

_________________________________

TODAY DID I...

○ SMILE

○ MEDITATE

○ EXERCISE

○ EAT NUTRITIOUS FOOD

○ CATCH FRESH AIR

○ SPEND TIME WITH THE
   PEOPLE I LOVE

○ SLEEP WELL

THREE THINGS I AM GRATEFUL FOR

_________________________________

_________________________________

_________________________________

_________________________________

_________________________________

I APPRECIATE MYSELF FOR

DID ANYTHING TRIGGER MY ANXIETY TODAY?

HOW DID I DEAL WITH IT?

HOW CAN I REFRAME MY ANXIOUS THOUGHTS TO FEEL BETTER?

THE BEST THING ABOUT TODAY

WHAT AM I EXCITED ABOUT FOR TOMORROW?

HOW WELL DID I MANAGE MY ANXIETY TODAY?

☆ ☆ ☆ ☆ ☆

# Tuesday

DATE:

TODAY I FELT

## WHAT WAS ON MY MIND TODAY? HOW DID IT MAKE ME FEEL?

_______________________________________________

_______________________________________________

_______________________________________________

_______________________________________________

_______________________________________________

## WHAT WENT WELL TODAY?

_________________________________

_________________________________

_________________________________

_________________________________

_________________________________

_________________________________

_________________________________

_________________________________

## TODAY DID I...

- ○ SMILE
- ○ MEDITATE
- ○ EXERCISE
- ○ EAT NUTRITIOUS FOOD
- ○ CATCH FRESH AIR
- ○ SPEND TIME WITH THE PEOPLE I LOVE
- ○ SLEEP WELL

## THREE THINGS I AM GRATEFUL FOR

_________________________________

_________________________________

_________________________________

_________________________________

_________________________________

## I APPRECIATE MYSELF FOR

DID ANYTHING TRIGGER MY ANXIETY TODAY?

_________________________________________________

_________________________________________________

_________________________________________________

_________________________________________________

HOW DID I DEAL WITH IT?

_________________________________________________

_________________________________________________

_________________________________________________

_________________________________________________

_________________________________________________

HOW CAN I REFRAME MY ANXIOUS THOUGHTS TO FEEL BETTER?

_________________________________________________

_________________________________________________

_________________________________________________

_________________________________________________

_________________________________________________

THE BEST THING ABOUT TODAY

____________________________

____________________________

____________________________

____________________________

____________________________

____________________________

WHAT AM I EXCITED ABOUT FOR TOMORROW?

HOW WELL DID I MANAGE MY ANXIETY TODAY?

☆ ☆ ☆ ☆ ☆

# Wednesday

DATE:

TODAY I FELT

## WHAT WAS ON MY MIND TODAY? HOW DID IT MAKE ME FEEL?

## WHAT WENT WELL TODAY?

## TODAY DID I...

- ○ SMILE
- ○ MEDITATE
- ○ EXERCISE
- ○ EAT NUTRITIOUS FOOD
- ○ CATCH FRESH AIR
- ○ SPEND TIME WITH THE PEOPLE I LOVE
- ○ SLEEP WELL

## THREE THINGS I AM GRATEFUL FOR

## I APPRECIATE MYSELF FOR

DID ANYTHING TRIGGER MY ANXIETY TODAY?

_______________________________________________

_______________________________________________

_______________________________________________

_______________________________________________

_______________________________________________

HOW DID I DEAL WITH IT?

_______________________________________________

_______________________________________________

_______________________________________________

_______________________________________________

_______________________________________________

HOW CAN I REFRAME MY ANXIOUS THOUGHTS TO FEEL BETTER?

_______________________________________________

_______________________________________________

_______________________________________________

_______________________________________________

_______________________________________________

THE BEST THING ABOUT TODAY

_______________________________

_______________________________

_______________________________

_______________________________

_______________________________

_______________________________

WHAT AM I EXCITED ABOUT FOR TOMORROW?

HOW WELL DID I MANAGE MY ANXIETY TODAY?

☆ ☆ ☆ ☆ ☆

#  Thursday

DATE:

TODAY I FELT

## WHAT WAS ON MY MIND TODAY? HOW DID IT MAKE ME FEEL?

___________________________________________

___________________________________________

___________________________________________

___________________________________________

___________________________________________

## WHAT WENT WELL TODAY?

_____________________________

_____________________________

_____________________________

_____________________________

_____________________________

_____________________________

_____________________________

_____________________________

## TODAY DID I...

- ○ SMILE
- ○ MEDITATE
- ○ EXERCISE
- ○ EAT NUTRITIOUS FOOD
- ○ CATCH FRESH AIR
- ○ SPEND TIME WITH THE PEOPLE I LOVE
- ○ SLEEP WELL

## THREE THINGS I AM GRATEFUL FOR

_____________________________

_____________________________

_____________________________

_____________________________

_____________________________

## I APPRECIATE MYSELF FOR

DID ANYTHING TRIGGER MY ANXIETY TODAY?

_______________________________________________

_______________________________________________

_______________________________________________

_______________________________________________

HOW DID I DEAL WITH IT?

_______________________________________________

_______________________________________________

_______________________________________________

_______________________________________________

HOW CAN I REFRAME MY ANXIOUS THOUGHTS TO FEEL BETTER?

_______________________________________________

_______________________________________________

_______________________________________________

_______________________________________________

THE BEST THING ABOUT TODAY

_______________________________

_______________________________

_______________________________

_______________________________

_______________________________

_______________________________

WHAT AM I EXCITED ABOUT FOR TOMORROW?

HOW WELL DID I MANAGE MY ANXIETY TODAY?

☆ ☆ ☆ ☆ ☆

# Friday

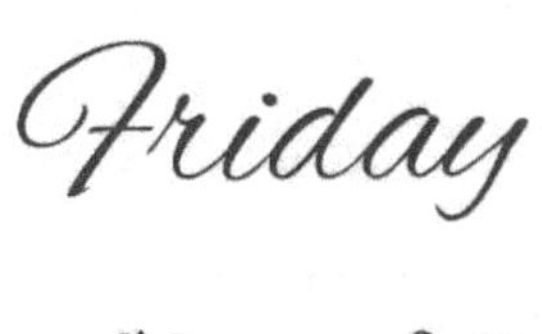

DATE:

TODAY I FELT

## WHAT WAS ON MY MIND TODAY? HOW DID IT MAKE ME FEEL?

_______________________________________________

_______________________________________________

_______________________________________________

_______________________________________________

## WHAT WENT WELL TODAY?

_____________________________

_____________________________

_____________________________

_____________________________

_____________________________

_____________________________

_____________________________

## TODAY DID I...

○ SMILE

○ MEDITATE

○ EXERCISE

○ EAT NUTRITIOUS FOOD

○ CATCH FRESH AIR

○ SPEND TIME WITH THE PEOPLE I LOVE

○ SLEEP WELL

## THREE THINGS I AM GRATEFUL FOR

_____________________________

_____________________________

_____________________________

_____________________________

_____________________________

## I APPRECIATE MYSELF FOR

DID ANYTHING TRIGGER MY ANXIETY TODAY?

_______________________________________________

_______________________________________________

_______________________________________________

_______________________________________________

HOW DID I DEAL WITH IT?

_______________________________________________

_______________________________________________

_______________________________________________

_______________________________________________

HOW CAN I REFRAME MY ANXIOUS THOUGHTS TO FEEL BETTER?

_______________________________________________

_______________________________________________

_______________________________________________

_______________________________________________

THE BEST THING ABOUT TODAY

_________________________________

_________________________________

_________________________________

_________________________________

_________________________________

WHAT AM I EXCITED ABOUT FOR TOMORROW?

HOW WELL DID I MANAGE MY ANXIETY TODAY?

☆ ☆ ☆ ☆ ☆

# Saturday

DATE:

TODAY I FELT

## WHAT WAS ON MY MIND TODAY? HOW DID IT MAKE ME FEEL?

## WHAT WENT WELL TODAY?

## TODAY DID I...

- ○ SMILE
- ○ MEDITATE
- ○ EXERCISE
- ○ EAT NUTRITIOUS FOOD
- ○ CATCH FRESH AIR
- ○ SPEND TIME WITH THE PEOPLE I LOVE
- ○ SLEEP WELL

## THREE THINGS I AM GRATEFUL FOR

## I APPRECIATE MYSELF FOR

DID ANYTHING TRIGGER MY ANXIETY TODAY?

HOW DID I DEAL WITH IT?

HOW CAN I REFRAME MY ANXIOUS THOUGHTS TO FEEL BETTER?

THE BEST THING ABOUT TODAY

WHAT AM I EXCITED ABOUT FOR TOMORROW?

HOW WELL DID I MANAGE MY ANXIETY TODAY?

☆ ☆ ☆ ☆ ☆

# Sunday

DATE:

TODAY I FELT

WHAT WAS ON MY MIND TODAY? HOW DID IT MAKE ME FEEL?

________________________________________

________________________________________

________________________________________

________________________________________

## WHAT WENT WELL TODAY?

________________________________

________________________________

________________________________

________________________________

________________________________

________________________________

________________________________

________________________________

## TODAY DID I...

○ SMILE

○ MEDITATE

○ EXERCISE

○ EAT NUTRITIOUS FOOD

○ CATCH FRESH AIR

○ SPEND TIME WITH THE
PEOPLE I LOVE

○ SLEEP WELL

## THREE THINGS I AM GRATEFUL FOR

________________________________

________________________________

________________________________

________________________________

________________________________

## I APPRECIATE MYSELF FOR

DID ANYTHING TRIGGER MY ANXIETY TODAY?

________________________________________

________________________________________

________________________________________

________________________________________

HOW DID I DEAL WITH IT?

________________________________________

________________________________________

________________________________________

________________________________________

________________________________________

HOW CAN I REFRAME MY ANXIOUS THOUGHTS TO FEEL BETTER?

________________________________________

________________________________________

________________________________________

________________________________________

THE BEST THING ABOUT TODAY

________________________________

________________________________

________________________________

________________________________

________________________________

________________________________

WHAT AM I EXCITED ABOUT FOR TOMORROW?

HOW WELL DID I MANAGE MY ANXIETY TODAY?

☆ ☆ ☆ ☆ ☆

# Week 1
# Check in

**WHAT DID I DO WELL THIS WEEK?**

______________________________________________

______________________________________________

______________________________________________

______________________________________________

**THIS WEEK I FELT**

**HOW WELL DID I MANAGE MY ANXIETY THIS WEEK?**

☆ ☆ ☆ ☆ ☆

**WHAT DID I DO WELL THIS WEEK?**

______________________________________________

______________________________________________

______________________________________________

______________________________________________

**WHAT WOULD I LIKE TO DO BETTER NEXT WEEK?**

**WHAT AM I EXCITED ABOUT IN THE UPCOMING WEEK?**

# Connect with Your Reason

"

WHAT WE PERCEIVE ABOUT OURSELVES IS GREATLY A REFLECTION OF HOW WE WILL END UP LIVING OUR LIVES

– STEPHEN RICHARDS

# Connect With Your Reason

Everything we do is driven by a purpose. If you desire to work on managing your anxiety, it is crucial to connect with the underlying reasons that motivate you. When you have a clear understanding of your personal "why", the "how" of managing anxiety will naturally fall into place.

Human beings are primarily driven by two fundamental reasons: the pursuit of pleasure or the avoidance of pain. Our decision-making process is often influenced by these underlying unconscious motivations that are shaped by our experiences and the lessons we have learned throughout our lives.

For example, let's say you have to meet with Person A. You may find that you don't feel particularly inclined to see them, and the mere thought of meeting them makes you feel unenthusiastic or stressed. In contrast, there is Person B, someone you deeply cherish and enjoy being with. Your love for Person B is so strong that you don't require any external motivation to meet them. Regardless of how tired or busy you may already be, you willingly make space for them in your schedule.

What do you think might be responsible for this difference in your response?

You might hold the belief that spending time with Person A will lead you away from pleasure and towards pain, while spending time with Person B will have the opposite effect. This unconscious assessment of the potential pain or pleasure we anticipate plays a significant role in guiding our actions and decisions.

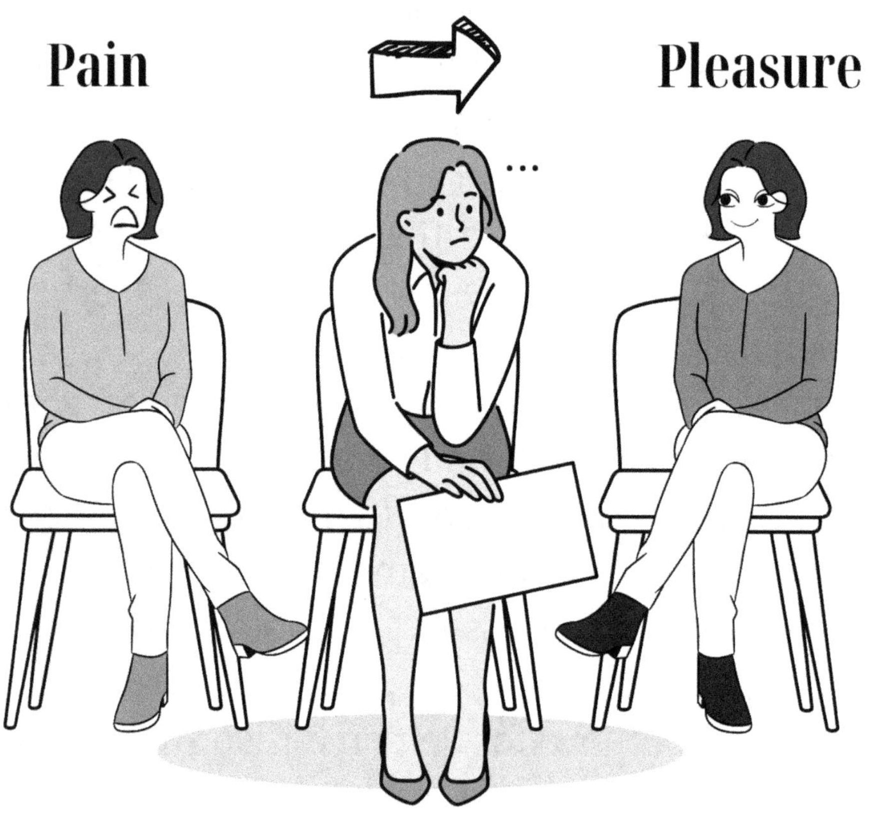


Hence, if your goal is to get rid of your anxiety you need to connect with the reason behind wanting to do so in terms of the pleasure you will get out of it and the pain you will move away from.

# The Pain Pleasure Equation

Do you want to get rid of your anxiety to avoid potential pain?

---

---

---

Elaborate on the pain you want to get rid of.

---

---

---

Do you want to get rid of your anxiety as you want to gain pleasure?

---

---

---

Elaborate on the pleasure you want to get.

---

---

---

# If you were to be calm and relaxed...

Name 3 undesirable things that will go away from your life. Draw them in the space below.

Name 3 desirable things that will come into your life. Draw them in the space below.

*Now focus more on what is desirable!*

# Visualization exercise

Create a beautiful picture in your mind of the kind of life you will be leading if you were to get rid of your anxiety and develop ways to stay calm despite challenges.

Visualize this as vividly as possible. Keep this visualization front and center of your mind in your daily life. It will keep you going even on days you are feeling overwhelmed.

# Reflect

How will getting rid of your anxiety transform your life?

_______________________________

_______________________________

_______________________________

How will it affect your relationships?

_______________________________

_______________________________

_______________________________

How will you enjoy your time once the anxiety is gone?

_______________________________

_______________________________

_______________________________

_______________________________

# Let's Color

# Monday

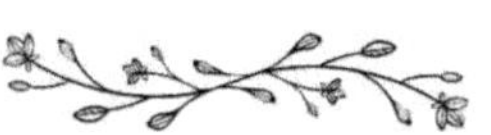

DATE:

TODAY I FELT

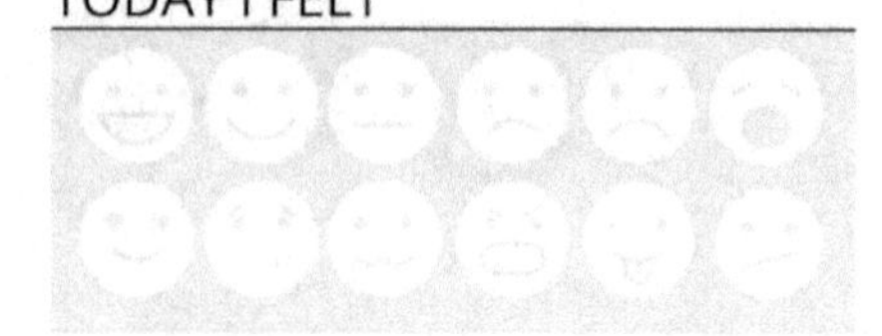

## WHAT WAS ON MY MIND TODAY? HOW DID IT MAKE ME FEEL?

---

## WHAT WENT WELL TODAY?

## TODAY DID I...

- ○ SMILE
- ○ MEDITATE
- ○ EXERCISE
- ○ EAT NUTRITIOUS FOOD
- ○ CATCH FRESH AIR
- ○ SPEND TIME WITH THE PEOPLE I LOVE
- ○ SLEEP WELL

## THREE THINGS I AM GRATEFUL FOR

## I APPRECIATE MYSELF FOR

DID ANYTHING TRIGGER MY ANXIETY TODAY?

HOW DID I DEAL WITH IT?

HOW CAN I REFRAME MY ANXIOUS THOUGHTS TO FEEL BETTER?

THE BEST THING ABOUT TODAY

WHAT AM I EXCITED ABOUT FOR TOMORROW?

HOW WELL DID I MANAGE MY ANXIETY TODAY?

☆ ☆ ☆ ☆ ☆

# Tuesday

DATE:

TODAY I FELT

WHAT WAS ON MY MIND TODAY? HOW DID IT MAKE ME FEEL?

_______________________________________________

_______________________________________________

_______________________________________________

_______________________________________________

## WHAT WENT WELL TODAY?

_____________________________________

_____________________________________

_____________________________________

_____________________________________

_____________________________________

_____________________________________

_____________________________________

_____________________________________

## TODAY DID I...

- ○ SMILE

- ○ MEDITATE

- ○ EXERCISE

- ○ EAT NUTRITIOUS FOOD

- ○ CATCH FRESH AIR

- ○ SPEND TIME WITH THE PEOPLE I LOVE

- ○ SLEEP WELL

## THREE THINGS I AM GRATEFUL FOR

_____________________________________

_____________________________________

_____________________________________

_____________________________________

_____________________________________

_____________________________________

## I APPRECIATE MYSELF FOR

DID ANYTHING TRIGGER MY ANXIETY TODAY?

_______________________________________

_______________________________________

_______________________________________

_______________________________________

HOW DID I DEAL WITH IT?

_______________________________________

_______________________________________

_______________________________________

_______________________________________

HOW CAN I REFRAME MY ANXIOUS THOUGHTS TO FEEL BETTER?

_______________________________________

_______________________________________

_______________________________________

_______________________________________

THE BEST THING ABOUT TODAY

_______________________________

_______________________________

_______________________________

_______________________________

_______________________________

_______________________________

WHAT AM I EXCITED ABOUT FOR TOMORROW?

HOW WELL DID I MANAGE MY ANXIETY TODAY?

☆ ☆ ☆ ☆ ☆

# Wednesday

DATE:

TODAY I FELT

WHAT WAS ON MY MIND TODAY? HOW DID IT MAKE ME FEEL?

_______________________________________________

_______________________________________________

_______________________________________________

_______________________________________________

_______________________________________________

## WHAT WENT WELL TODAY?

_____________________________________

_____________________________________

_____________________________________

_____________________________________

_____________________________________

_____________________________________

_____________________________________

## TODAY DID I...

○ SMILE

○ MEDITATE

○ EXERCISE

○ EAT NUTRITIOUS FOOD

○ CATCH FRESH AIR

○ SPEND TIME WITH THE
PEOPLE I LOVE

○ SLEEP WELL

## THREE THINGS I AM GRATEFUL FOR

_____________________________________

_____________________________________

_____________________________________

_____________________________________

_____________________________________

## I APPRECIATE MYSELF FOR

DID ANYTHING TRIGGER MY ANXIETY TODAY?

_______________________________________________

_______________________________________________

_______________________________________________

_______________________________________________

_______________________________________________

HOW DID I DEAL WITH IT?

_______________________________________________

_______________________________________________

_______________________________________________

_______________________________________________

_______________________________________________

HOW CAN I REFRAME MY ANXIOUS THOUGHTS TO FEEL BETTER?

_______________________________________________

_______________________________________________

_______________________________________________

_______________________________________________

_______________________________________________

THE BEST THING ABOUT TODAY

WHAT AM I EXCITED ABOUT FOR TOMORROW?

HOW WELL DID I MANAGE MY ANXIETY TODAY?

☆ ☆ ☆ ☆ ☆

# Thursday

DATE:

TODAY I FELT

## WHAT WAS ON MY MIND TODAY? HOW DID IT MAKE ME FEEL?

## WHAT WENT WELL TODAY?

## TODAY DID I...

- ○ SMILE
- ○ MEDITATE
- ○ EXERCISE
- ○ EAT NUTRITIOUS FOOD
- ○ CATCH FRESH AIR
- ○ SPEND TIME WITH THE PEOPLE I LOVE
- ○ SLEEP WELL

## THREE THINGS I AM GRATEFUL FOR

## I APPRECIATE MYSELF FOR

DID ANYTHING TRIGGER MY ANXIETY TODAY?

HOW DID I DEAL WITH IT?

HOW CAN I REFRAME MY ANXIOUS THOUGHTS TO FEEL BETTER?

THE BEST THING ABOUT TODAY

WHAT AM I EXCITED ABOUT FOR TOMORROW?

HOW WELL DID I MANAGE MY ANXIETY TODAY?
☆ ☆ ☆ ☆ ☆

# Friday

DATE:

TODAY I FELT
_______________________

WHAT WAS ON MY MIND TODAY? HOW DID IT MAKE ME FEEL?

___________________________________________

___________________________________________

___________________________________________

___________________________________________

WHAT WENT WELL TODAY?

_______________________________

_______________________________

_______________________________

_______________________________

_______________________________

_______________________________

_______________________________

TODAY DID I...

○ SMILE

○ MEDITATE

○ EXERCISE

○ EAT NUTRITIOUS FOOD

○ CATCH FRESH AIR

○ SPEND TIME WITH THE PEOPLE I LOVE

○ SLEEP WELL

THREE THINGS I AM GRATEFUL FOR

_______________________________

_______________________________

_______________________________

_______________________________

I APPRECIATE MYSELF FOR

DID ANYTHING TRIGGER MY ANXIETY TODAY?

_______________________________________________

_______________________________________________

_______________________________________________

_______________________________________________

HOW DID I DEAL WITH IT?

_______________________________________________

_______________________________________________

_______________________________________________

_______________________________________________

HOW CAN I REFRAME MY ANXIOUS THOUGHTS TO FEEL BETTER?

_______________________________________________

_______________________________________________

_______________________________________________

_______________________________________________

THE BEST THING ABOUT TODAY

_______________________________

_______________________________

_______________________________

_______________________________

_______________________________

WHAT AM I EXCITED ABOUT FOR TOMORROW?




HOW WELL DID I MANAGE MY ANXIETY TODAY?

☆ ☆ ☆ ☆ ☆

# Saturday

DATE:

TODAY I FELT

---

## WHAT WAS ON MY MIND TODAY? HOW DID IT MAKE ME FEEL?

---

## WHAT WENT WELL TODAY?

## TODAY DID I...

- ○ SMILE
- ○ MEDITATE
- ○ EXERCISE
- ○ EAT NUTRITIOUS FOOD
- ○ CATCH FRESH AIR
- ○ SPEND TIME WITH THE PEOPLE I LOVE
- ○ SLEEP WELL

## THREE THINGS I AM GRATEFUL FOR

## I APPRECIATE MYSELF FOR

DID ANYTHING TRIGGER MY ANXIETY TODAY?

_______________________________________

_______________________________________

_______________________________________

_______________________________________

_______________________________________

HOW DID I DEAL WITH IT?

_______________________________________

_______________________________________

_______________________________________

_______________________________________

_______________________________________

HOW CAN I REFRAME MY ANXIOUS THOUGHTS TO FEEL BETTER?

_______________________________________

_______________________________________

_______________________________________

_______________________________________

_______________________________________

THE BEST THING ABOUT TODAY

___________________________

___________________________

___________________________

___________________________

___________________________

___________________________

WHAT AM I EXCITED ABOUT FOR TOMORROW?

HOW WELL DID I MANAGE MY ANXIETY TODAY?

☆ ☆ ☆ ☆ ☆

# Sunday

DATE:

TODAY I FELT

WHAT WAS ON MY MIND TODAY? HOW DID IT MAKE ME FEEL?

_______________________________________________

_______________________________________________

_______________________________________________

_______________________________________________

_______________________________________________

## WHAT WENT WELL TODAY?

_________________________________

_________________________________

_________________________________

_________________________________

_________________________________

_________________________________

_________________________________

_________________________________

_________________________________

## TODAY DID I...

○ SMILE

○ MEDITATE

○ EXERCISE

○ EAT NUTRITIOUS FOOD

○ CATCH FRESH AIR

○ SPEND TIME WITH THE
PEOPLE I LOVE

○ SLEEP WELL

## THREE THINGS I AM GRATEFUL FOR

_________________________________

_________________________________

_________________________________

_________________________________

_________________________________

_________________________________

## I APPRECIATE MYSELF FOR

DID ANYTHING TRIGGER MY ANXIETY TODAY?

HOW DID I DEAL WITH IT?

HOW CAN I REFRAME MY ANXIOUS THOUGHTS TO FEEL BETTER?

THE BEST THING ABOUT TODAY

WHAT AM I EXCITED ABOUT FOR TOMORROW?

HOW WELL DID I MANAGE MY ANXIETY TODAY?

☆ ☆ ☆ ☆ ☆

# Week 2 Check in

DATE:

WHAT DID I DO WELL THIS WEEK?

_______________________________________________

_______________________________________________

_______________________________________________

_______________________________________________

THIS WEEK I FELT

HOW WELL DID I MANAGE MY ANXIETY THIS WEEK?

WHAT DID I DO WELL THIS WEEK?

_______________________________________________

_______________________________________________

_______________________________________________

_______________________________________________

WHAT WOULD I LIKE TO DO BETTER NEXT WEEK?

WHAT AM I EXCITED ABOUT IN THE UPCOMING WEEK?

# Thought Feeling Behavior

"

THE THREAT OF THE ATTACK IS GREATER THAN THE ATTACK ITSELF

# Thought Feeling Behavior

Let's delve into the starting point of anxiety. The experience of feeling anxious is preceded by specific thoughts. These thoughts are triggered by events or circumstances. For example, if you have lost an important document, you might feel anxious about the potential consequences. These thoughts then give rise to the feeling of anxiety, which subsequently influences your behavior. This behavior could manifest as rumination, compulsive searching for the document, or withdrawal to your room.

The triggers for anxiety are not limited to external factors; they can also originate from within us. Sometimes, despite everything going well, we can generate hypothetical scenarios that lead to anxiety. For example, consider a situation where you haven't lost a document, but you start imagining the potential consequences of losing it. This trigger is internal, imaginary, and self-created. It is often based on fear. The visualized scenarios may not reflect the reality of the current situation but can significantly impact our emotional state.

By being aware of this, we can begin to differentiate between genuine concerns and anxiety-inducing thoughts that arise from our imagination.

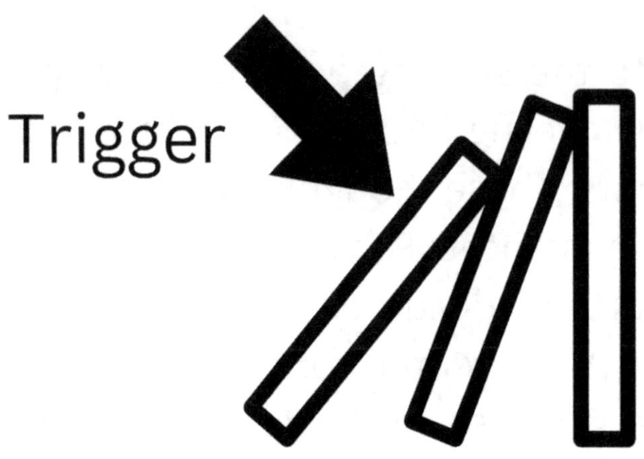


Notice what the trigger does to your thinking. How do you feel as a result of those thoughts? What do you do then?

For example, I made a mistake in an important presentation. I'm certain that everyone will notice it, and they will laugh at me behind my back. These negative thoughts can have a detrimental impact on my performance, leading to more mistakes during the presentation.

To effectively deal with this situation, I can catch myself when I begin entertaining negative thoughts and consciously replace them with positive ones, such as: "It's okay to make mistakes. Everyone makes mistakes from time to time. Making errors is a part of being human."

These thoughts will put me in a more positive mindset, allowing me to regain my focus and deliver the remaining part of the presentation with utmost effort.

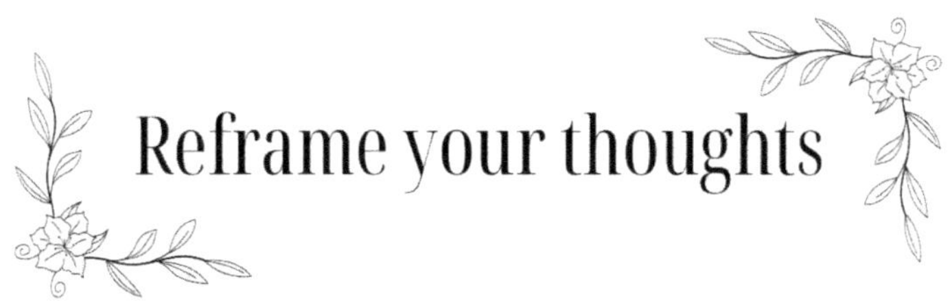

# Reframe your thoughts

It is easy to get carried away in the flow of automatic negative thoughts when something triggers us. Taking a step back and reframing our thoughts into positive ones can enhance our performance in anxiety-inducing situations.

If something happens that triggers anxiety, take a moment to consider if there is a potential for learning from the situation.

Is there an opportunity to improve your skills or develop new capabilities? Will the process of developing those skills and confronting your fears make you stronger? Can this experience teach you valuable lessons that you would have otherwise missed?

Thinking about the benefits of confronting your fears can shift your focus from fearing what you don't want to becoming excited about what you *do* want.

# Getting to the source

Think of a situation that triggers anxiety in you and answer the following questions.

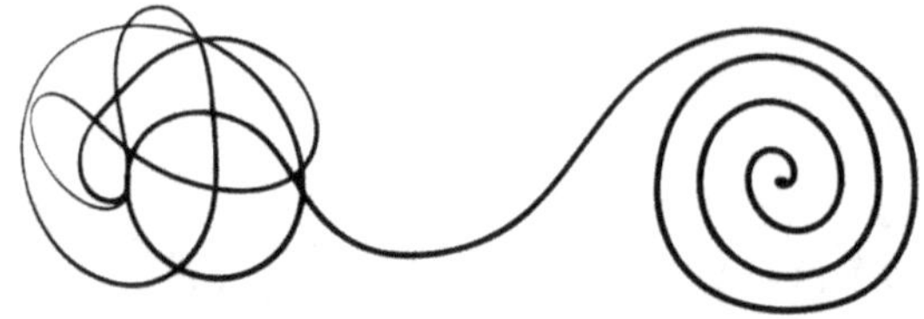

What specific thoughts come to mind when you think about this situation?

How do these thoughts make you feel?

How do these feelings impact your behavior or performance in such situations?

What can you learn from it if you were to take it up as a challenge head-on?

_________________________________________________

_________________________________________________

_________________________________________________

How will it improve your skills and capabilities?

_________________________________________________

_________________________________________________

_________________________________________________

Will facing this fear and conquering it make you more confident?

_________________________________________________

_________________________________________________

_________________________________________________

How would these new feelings influence your behavior or performance?

_________________________________________________

_________________________________________________

_________________________________________________

# Replace anxiety with excitement

Feeling a little anxious about what is going to happen can actually be a good thing. It prompts us to work hard and take action. It is only when we become paralyzed by anxiety that we miss out on life. Once we become excited about what we can achieve by overcoming our anxiety it becomes easier to do so.

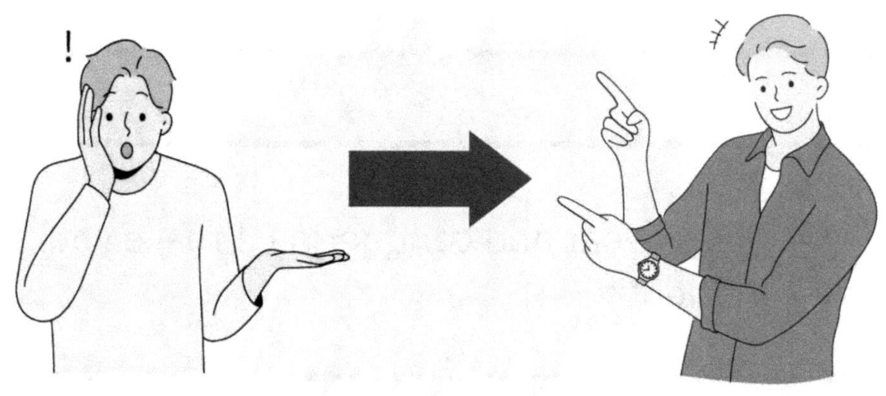

Pro Tip

If replacing anxiety with excitement is challenging, try pretending to be excited. Interestingly, our brain cannot distinguish between excitement and anxiety at a physiological level, making it a helpful technique to shift our mindset.

# Let's Color

# Monday

DATE:

TODAY I FELT
___________________________

## WHAT WAS ON MY MIND TODAY? HOW DID IT MAKE ME FEEL?

_______________________________________________

_______________________________________________

_______________________________________________

_______________________________________________

## WHAT WENT WELL TODAY?

_________________________________

_________________________________

_________________________________

_________________________________

_________________________________

_________________________________

_________________________________

_________________________________

## TODAY DID I...

○ SMILE

○ MEDITATE

○ EXERCISE

○ EAT NUTRITIOUS FOOD

○ CATCH FRESH AIR

○ SPEND TIME WITH THE
  PEOPLE I LOVE

○ SLEEP WELL

## THREE THINGS I AM GRATEFUL FOR

_________________________________

_________________________________

_________________________________

_________________________________

## I APPRECIATE MYSELF FOR

DID ANYTHING TRIGGER MY ANXIETY TODAY?

HOW DID I DEAL WITH IT?

HOW CAN I REFRAME MY ANXIOUS THOUGHTS TO FEEL BETTER?

THE BEST THING ABOUT TODAY

WHAT AM I EXCITED ABOUT FOR TOMORROW?

HOW WELL DID I MANAGE MY ANXIETY TODAY?

DATE:

TODAY I FELT

## WHAT WAS ON MY MIND TODAY? HOW DID IT MAKE ME FEEL?

## WHAT WENT WELL TODAY?

## TODAY DID I...

○ SMILE

○ MEDITATE

○ EXERCISE

○ EAT NUTRITIOUS FOOD

○ CATCH FRESH AIR

○ SPEND TIME WITH THE PEOPLE I LOVE

○ SLEEP WELL

## THREE THINGS I AM GRATEFUL FOR

## I APPRECIATE MYSELF FOR

DID ANYTHING TRIGGER MY ANXIETY TODAY?

HOW DID I DEAL WITH IT?

HOW CAN I REFRAME MY ANXIOUS THOUGHTS TO FEEL BETTER?

THE BEST THING ABOUT TODAY

WHAT AM I EXCITED ABOUT FOR TOMORROW?

HOW WELL DID I MANAGE MY ANXIETY TODAY?

☆ ☆ ☆ ☆ ☆

# Wednesday

DATE:

TODAY I FELT

WHAT WAS ON MY MIND TODAY? HOW DID IT MAKE ME FEEL?

_______________________________________________
_______________________________________________
_______________________________________________
_______________________________________________
_______________________________________________

WHAT WENT WELL TODAY?

_____________________________
_____________________________
_____________________________
_____________________________
_____________________________
_____________________________
_____________________________
_____________________________

TODAY DID I...

○ SMILE

○ MEDITATE

○ EXERCISE

○ EAT NUTRITIOUS FOOD

○ CATCH FRESH AIR

○ SPEND TIME WITH THE
PEOPLE I LOVE

○ SLEEP WELL

THREE THINGS I AM GRATEFUL FOR

_____________________________
_____________________________
_____________________________
_____________________________
_____________________________

I APPRECIATE MYSELF FOR

DID ANYTHING TRIGGER MY ANXIETY TODAY?

HOW DID I DEAL WITH IT?

HOW CAN I REFRAME MY ANXIOUS THOUGHTS TO FEEL BETTER?

THE BEST THING ABOUT TODAY

WHAT AM I EXCITED ABOUT FOR TOMORROW?

HOW WELL DID I MANAGE MY ANXIETY TODAY?

☆ ☆ ☆ ☆ ☆

# Thursday

DATE:

TODAY I FELT

WHAT WAS ON MY MIND TODAY? HOW DID IT MAKE ME FEEL?

_______________________________________________

_______________________________________________

_______________________________________________

_______________________________________________

WHAT WENT WELL TODAY?

_________________________________

_________________________________

_________________________________

_________________________________

_________________________________

_________________________________

_________________________________

_________________________________

TODAY DID I...

○ SMILE

○ MEDITATE

○ EXERCISE

○ EAT NUTRITIOUS FOOD

○ CATCH FRESH AIR

○ SPEND TIME WITH THE
  PEOPLE I LOVE

○ SLEEP WELL

THREE THINGS I AM GRATEFUL FOR

_________________________________

_________________________________

_________________________________

_________________________________

_________________________________

I APPRECIATE MYSELF FOR

DID ANYTHING TRIGGER MY ANXIETY TODAY?

HOW DID I DEAL WITH IT?

HOW CAN I REFRAME MY ANXIOUS THOUGHTS TO FEEL BETTER?

THE BEST THING ABOUT TODAY

WHAT AM I EXCITED ABOUT FOR TOMORROW?

HOW WELL DID I MANAGE MY ANXIETY TODAY?
☆ ☆ ☆ ☆ ☆

# Friday

DATE:

TODAY I FELT

WHAT WAS ON MY MIND TODAY? HOW DID IT MAKE ME FEEL?

_______________________________________________

_______________________________________________

_______________________________________________

_______________________________________________

_______________________________________________

## WHAT WENT WELL TODAY?

_________________________________

_________________________________

_________________________________

_________________________________

_________________________________

_________________________________

_________________________________

_________________________________

_________________________________

## TODAY DID I...

- ○ SMILE
- ○ MEDITATE
- ○ EXERCISE
- ○ EAT NUTRITIOUS FOOD
- ○ CATCH FRESH AIR
- ○ SPEND TIME WITH THE PEOPLE I LOVE
- ○ SLEEP WELL

## THREE THINGS I AM GRATEFUL FOR

_________________________________

_________________________________

_________________________________

_________________________________

_________________________________

_________________________________

## I APPRECIATE MYSELF FOR

DID ANYTHING TRIGGER MY ANXIETY TODAY?

_______________________________________

_______________________________________

_______________________________________

_______________________________________

HOW DID I DEAL WITH IT?

_______________________________________

_______________________________________

_______________________________________

_______________________________________

HOW CAN I REFRAME MY ANXIOUS THOUGHTS TO FEEL BETTER?

_______________________________________

_______________________________________

_______________________________________

_______________________________________

THE BEST THING ABOUT TODAY

_________________________________

_________________________________

_________________________________

_________________________________

_________________________________

_________________________________

_________________________________

WHAT AM I EXCITED ABOUT FOR TOMORROW?

HOW WELL DID I MANAGE MY ANXIETY TODAY?

☆ ☆ ☆ ☆ ☆

# Saturday

DATE:

TODAY I FELT

WHAT WAS ON MY MIND TODAY? HOW DID IT MAKE ME FEEL?

WHAT WENT WELL TODAY?

## TODAY DID I...

- ○ SMILE
- ○ MEDITATE
- ○ EXERCISE
- ○ EAT NUTRITIOUS FOOD
- ○ CATCH FRESH AIR
- ○ SPEND TIME WITH THE PEOPLE I LOVE
- ○ SLEEP WELL

THREE THINGS I AM GRATEFUL FOR

I APPRECIATE MYSELF FOR

DID ANYTHING TRIGGER MY ANXIETY TODAY?

_____________________________________________

_____________________________________________

_____________________________________________

_____________________________________________

HOW DID I DEAL WITH IT?

_____________________________________________

_____________________________________________

_____________________________________________

_____________________________________________

HOW CAN I REFRAME MY ANXIOUS THOUGHTS TO FEEL BETTER?

_____________________________________________

_____________________________________________

_____________________________________________

_____________________________________________

THE BEST THING ABOUT TODAY

WHAT AM I EXCITED ABOUT FOR TOMORROW?

HOW WELL DID I MANAGE MY ANXIETY TODAY?

☆ ☆ ☆ ☆ ☆

# Sunday

DATE:

TODAY I FELT

WHAT WAS ON MY MIND TODAY? HOW DID IT MAKE ME FEEL?

_______________________________________________

_______________________________________________

_______________________________________________

_______________________________________________

_______________________________________________

## WHAT WENT WELL TODAY?

## TODAY DID I...

- ○ SMILE
- ○ MEDITATE
- ○ EXERCISE
- ○ EAT NUTRITIOUS FOOD
- ○ CATCH FRESH AIR
- ○ SPEND TIME WITH THE PEOPLE I LOVE
- ○ SLEEP WELL

## THREE THINGS I AM GRATEFUL FOR

## I APPRECIATE MYSELF FOR

DID ANYTHING TRIGGER MY ANXIETY TODAY?

_______________________________________

_______________________________________

_______________________________________

_______________________________________

HOW DID I DEAL WITH IT?

_______________________________________

_______________________________________

_______________________________________

_______________________________________

HOW CAN I REFRAME MY ANXIOUS THOUGHTS TO FEEL BETTER?

_______________________________________

_______________________________________

_______________________________________

_______________________________________

THE BEST THING ABOUT TODAY

_______________________

_______________________

_______________________

_______________________

_______________________

_______________________

WHAT AM I EXCITED ABOUT FOR TOMORROW?

HOW WELL DID I MANAGE MY ANXIETY TODAY?

☆ ☆ ☆ ☆ ☆

# Week 3 Check in

DATE:

WHAT DID I DO WELL THIS WEEK?

_______________________________________

_______________________________________

_______________________________________

_______________________________________

THIS WEEK I FELT

HOW WELL DID I MANAGE MY ANXIETY THIS WEEK?

WHAT DID I DO WELL THIS WEEK?

_______________________________________

_______________________________________

_______________________________________

_______________________________________

WHAT WOULD I LIKE TO DO BETTER NEXT WEEK?

WHAT AM I EXCITED ABOUT IN THE UPCOMING WEEK?

# Coping Mechanisms

> IT'S OKAY TO MAKE
MISTAKES. TO HAVE BAD
DAYS. TO BE LESS THAN
PERFECT. TO DO WHAT'S
BEST FOR YOURSELF.

# Coping Mechanisms

There are numerous ways in which we attempt to deflect the anxiety we experience, such as blaming others, expecting perfection, or exerting control. Although these strategies may provide temporary relief, they do not address the root cause of our problems. Instead, they serve as coping mechanisms that distract us from the underlying issues responsible for our anxiety.

## Perfectionism

Do you believe that a task must be executed flawlessly to be acceptable? Do you set high standards for yourself that are challenging to meet?

We often strive for perfection as a means of coping with anxiety. This happens when we believe that by exerting control over our environment and making it more predictable, we can manage the consequences better.

This desire for control manifests as an ongoing pursuit of perfection. It puts immense pressure on us, and we may experience anxiety when we fall short of those unrealistic standards. We hold a mental image of how things should be, and if this image is idealistic, the likelihood of it aligning perfectly with reality diminishes.

Consequently, we face a higher risk of disappointment when life unfolds differently, leading to anxiety.

The notion of a perfect mental image is ironic. If the image were genuinely perfect, it would adapt to the current situation rather than expecting the situation to conform to it. Since this mental picture remains unchanged, it becomes apparent that it isn't truly perfect after all.

*Anxiety arises when we doubt our ability to cope with difficult situations*

To be calm, it is important to have confidence in our ability to handle various scenarios. We can do this by planning for the best and being adaptable to whatever comes next.

Name 3 events/situations that usually trigger your anxiety.

_______________________________________

_______________________________________

_______________________________________

How does your behavior change when you are triggered?

_______________________________________

_______________________________________

_______________________________________

# How do you cope with your anxiety?

Do you tend to blame others when things don't happen as expected?   YES OR NO

Does blaming a situation or person outside make you feel better temporarily?   YES OR NO

Do you try to do tasks faster?   YES OR NO

Do you feel the need to do tasks perfectly?   YES OR NO

If the task doesn't happen perfectly do you feel disappointed for a long time?   YES OR NO

How well do you handle unexpected situations?

_______________________________________________

_______________________________________________

_______________________________________________

On a scale of 1 to 10, how important is it to you
that your life be predictable?

_______________________________________________

Do you try to control people around you so that
your situations become predictable?

_______________________________________________

_______________________________________________

_______________________________________________

Do you find yourself obsessively engaging in work,
shopping, cooking, binge eating, drinking, or any
other activities as a means of distracting yourself
from your anxiety? If so, elaborate on your
behavior.

_______________________________________________

_______________________________________________

_______________________________________________

Using your answers to the above questions do you think you deflect your anxiety by:

- Being perfect
- Being fast
- Being controlling
- Blaming someone
- Indulging in an activity obsessively
- Or something else? Please mention: ________

Write affirmations to counter the ones you identify with. Here are some examples:

Being perfect: *I am okay the way I am.*

___________________________________

Being fast: *I am doing the best I can.*

___________________________________

Being controlling: *I accept people and the choices they make.*

___________________________________

Blaming someone: *Everyone is doing the best they can.*

___________________________________

Indulging in an activity obsessively: *I can face my fears. I don't need a distraction.*

___________________________________

DATE:

TODAY I FELT

## WHAT WAS ON MY MIND TODAY? HOW DID IT MAKE ME FEEL?

_______________________________________________

_______________________________________________

_______________________________________________

_______________________________________________

_______________________________________________

## WHAT WENT WELL TODAY?

_________________________________

_________________________________

_________________________________

_________________________________

_________________________________

_________________________________

_________________________________

_________________________________

## TODAY DID I...

- ○ SMILE
- ○ MEDITATE
- ○ EXERCISE
- ○ EAT NUTRITIOUS FOOD
- ○ CATCH FRESH AIR
- ○ SPEND TIME WITH THE PEOPLE I LOVE
- ○ SLEEP WELL

## THREE THINGS I AM GRATEFUL FOR

_________________________________

_________________________________

_________________________________

_________________________________

_________________________________

_________________________________

## I APPRECIATE MYSELF FOR

DID ANYTHING TRIGGER MY ANXIETY TODAY?

HOW DID I DEAL WITH IT?

HOW CAN I REFRAME MY ANXIOUS THOUGHTS TO FEEL BETTER?

THE BEST THING ABOUT TODAY

WHAT AM I EXCITED ABOUT FOR TOMORROW?

HOW WELL DID I MANAGE MY ANXIETY TODAY?

☆ ☆ ☆ ☆ ☆

# Tuesday

DATE:

TODAY I FELT

WHAT WAS ON MY MIND TODAY? HOW DID IT MAKE ME FEEL?

_______________________________________________

_______________________________________________

_______________________________________________

_______________________________________________

WHAT WENT WELL TODAY?

_____________________________

_____________________________

_____________________________

_____________________________

_____________________________

_____________________________

_____________________________

_____________________________

TODAY DID I...

- ○ SMILE
- ○ MEDITATE
- ○ EXERCISE
- ○ EAT NUTRITIOUS FOOD
- ○ CATCH FRESH AIR
- ○ SPEND TIME WITH THE PEOPLE I LOVE
- ○ SLEEP WELL

THREE THINGS I AM GRATEFUL FOR

_____________________________

_____________________________

_____________________________

_____________________________

_____________________________

_____________________________

I APPRECIATE MYSELF FOR

DID ANYTHING TRIGGER MY ANXIETY TODAY?

HOW DID I DEAL WITH IT?

HOW CAN I REFRAME MY ANXIOUS THOUGHTS TO FEEL BETTER?

THE BEST THING ABOUT TODAY

WHAT AM I EXCITED ABOUT FOR TOMORROW?

HOW WELL DID I MANAGE MY ANXIETY TODAY?

☆ ☆ ☆ ☆ ☆

# Wednesday

DATE:

TODAY I FELT

WHAT WAS ON MY MIND TODAY? HOW DID IT MAKE ME FEEL?

_______________________________________________

_______________________________________________

_______________________________________________

_______________________________________________

_______________________________________________

## WHAT WENT WELL TODAY?

_______________________________

_______________________________

_______________________________

_______________________________

_______________________________

_______________________________

_______________________________

_______________________________

## TODAY DID I...

○ SMILE

○ MEDITATE

○ EXERCISE

○ EAT NUTRITIOUS FOOD

○ CATCH FRESH AIR

○ SPEND TIME WITH THE PEOPLE I LOVE

○ SLEEP WELL

## THREE THINGS I AM GRATEFUL FOR

_______________________________

_______________________________

_______________________________

_______________________________

_______________________________

## I APPRECIATE MYSELF FOR

DID ANYTHING TRIGGER MY ANXIETY TODAY?

_______________________________________________

_______________________________________________

_______________________________________________

_______________________________________________

HOW DID I DEAL WITH IT?

_______________________________________________

_______________________________________________

_______________________________________________

_______________________________________________

HOW CAN I REFRAME MY ANXIOUS THOUGHTS TO FEEL BETTER?

_______________________________________________

_______________________________________________

_______________________________________________

_______________________________________________

THE BEST THING ABOUT TODAY

WHAT AM I EXCITED ABOUT FOR TOMORROW?

HOW WELL DID I MANAGE MY ANXIETY TODAY?

☆ ☆ ☆ ☆ ☆

# Thursday

DATE:

TODAY I FELT

WHAT WAS ON MY MIND TODAY? HOW DID IT MAKE ME FEEL?

_______________________________________________

_______________________________________________

_______________________________________________

_______________________________________________

## WHAT WENT WELL TODAY?

_______________________________________

_______________________________________

_______________________________________

_______________________________________

_______________________________________

_______________________________________

_______________________________________

## TODAY DID I...

- ○ SMILE
- ○ MEDITATE
- ○ EXERCISE
- ○ EAT NUTRITIOUS FOOD
- ○ CATCH FRESH AIR
- ○ SPEND TIME WITH THE PEOPLE I LOVE
- ○ SLEEP WELL

## THREE THINGS I AM GRATEFUL FOR

_______________________________________

_______________________________________

_______________________________________

## I APPRECIATE MYSELF FOR

DID ANYTHING TRIGGER MY ANXIETY TODAY?

HOW DID I DEAL WITH IT?

HOW CAN I REFRAME MY ANXIOUS THOUGHTS TO FEEL BETTER?

THE BEST THING ABOUT TODAY

WHAT AM I EXCITED ABOUT FOR TOMORROW?

HOW WELL DID I MANAGE MY ANXIETY TODAY?

☆ ☆ ☆ ☆ ☆

# Friday

DATE:

TODAY I FELT

## WHAT WAS ON MY MIND TODAY? HOW DID IT MAKE ME FEEL?

## WHAT WENT WELL TODAY?

## TODAY DID I...

- ○ SMILE
- ○ MEDITATE
- ○ EXERCISE
- ○ EAT NUTRITIOUS FOOD
- ○ CATCH FRESH AIR
- ○ SPEND TIME WITH THE PEOPLE I LOVE
- ○ SLEEP WELL

## THREE THINGS I AM GRATEFUL FOR

## I APPRECIATE MYSELF FOR

DID ANYTHING TRIGGER MY ANXIETY TODAY?

HOW DID I DEAL WITH IT?

HOW CAN I REFRAME MY ANXIOUS THOUGHTS TO FEEL BETTER?

THE BEST THING ABOUT TODAY

WHAT AM I EXCITED ABOUT FOR TOMORROW?

HOW WELL DID I MANAGE MY ANXIETY TODAY?

☆ ☆ ☆ ☆ ☆

# Saturday

DATE:

TODAY I FELT

## WHAT WAS ON MY MIND TODAY? HOW DID IT MAKE ME FEEL?

______________________________

______________________________

______________________________

______________________________

## WHAT WENT WELL TODAY?

______________________________

______________________________

______________________________

______________________________

______________________________

______________________________

______________________________

______________________________

## TODAY DID I...

○ SMILE

○ MEDITATE

○ EXERCISE

○ EAT NUTRITIOUS FOOD

◉ CATCH FRESH AIR

○ SPEND TIME WITH THE PEOPLE I LOVE

○ SLEEP WELL

## THREE THINGS I AM GRATEFUL FOR

______________________________

______________________________

______________________________

## I APPRECIATE MYSELF FOR

DID ANYTHING TRIGGER MY ANXIETY TODAY?

HOW DID I DEAL WITH IT?

HOW CAN I REFRAME MY ANXIOUS THOUGHTS TO FEEL BETTER?

THE BEST THING ABOUT TODAY

WHAT AM I EXCITED ABOUT FOR TOMORROW?

HOW WELL DID I MANAGE MY ANXIETY TODAY?

☆ ☆ ☆ ☆ ☆

# Sunday

DATE:

TODAY I FELT
_______________________

## WHAT WAS ON MY MIND TODAY? HOW DID IT MAKE ME FEEL?

_________________________________________________

_________________________________________________

_________________________________________________

_________________________________________________

## WHAT WENT WELL TODAY?

_________________________________

_________________________________

_________________________________

_________________________________

_________________________________

_________________________________

_________________________________

_________________________________

## TODAY DID I...

- ○ SMILE

- ○ MEDITATE

- ○ EXERCISE

- ○ EAT NUTRITIOUS FOOD

- ○ CATCH FRESH AIR

- ○ SPEND TIME WITH THE PEOPLE I LOVE

- ○ SLEEP WELL

## THREE THINGS I AM GRATEFUL FOR

_________________________________

_________________________________

_________________________________

_________________________________

_________________________________

_________________________________

## I APPRECIATE MYSELF FOR

DID ANYTHING TRIGGER MY ANXIETY TODAY?

____________________________________

____________________________________

____________________________________

____________________________________

HOW DID I DEAL WITH IT?

____________________________________

____________________________________

____________________________________

____________________________________

HOW CAN I REFRAME MY ANXIOUS THOUGHTS TO FEEL BETTER?

____________________________________

____________________________________

____________________________________

____________________________________

THE BEST THING ABOUT TODAY

__________________________

__________________________

__________________________

__________________________

__________________________

__________________________

WHAT AM I EXCITED ABOUT FOR TOMORROW?

HOW WELL DID I MANAGE MY ANXIETY TODAY?

☆ ☆ ☆ ☆ ☆

# Week 4 Check in

## WHAT DID I DO WELL THIS WEEK?

________________________________________

________________________________________

________________________________________

________________________________________

## THIS WEEK I FELT

## HOW WELL DID I MANAGE MY ANXIETY THIS WEEK?

## WHAT DID I DO WELL THIS WEEK?

________________________________________

________________________________________

________________________________________

________________________________________

## WHAT WOULD I LIKE TO DO BETTER NEXT WEEK?

## WHAT AM I EXCITED ABOUT IN THE UPCOMING WEEK?

# Month 1 Check in

## HOW WELL DID I MANAGE MY ANXIETY THIS MONTH?

☆ ☆ ☆ ☆ ☆

## HOW DO I FEEL ABOUT THIS MONTH?

_______________________________________________

_______________________________________________

_______________________________________________

## MY ACCOMPLISHMENTS THIS MONTH

**1**      **2**      **3**

## WHAT HELPED ME STAY CALM THIS MONTH?

_______________________________________________

_______________________________________________

_______________________________________________

_______________________________________________

## HOW HAVE I GROWN THIS MONTH?

____________________

____________________

____________________

____________________

____________________

## WHAT DO I WANT TO DO DIFFERENTLY NEXT MONTH?

____________________

____________________

____________________

____________________

____________________

# Let's Color

# Mindfulness

"

YOU DON'T HAVE TO
FIGURE EVERYTHING OUT
AT ONCE. YOU CAN GET
THERE ONE STEP AT A TIME.

# Mindfulness

Our fast-paced life rarely allows us to be fully present at any given moment. Technological advancements enable people to reach us anywhere, leaving us with little opportunity to find solace.

We are constantly bombarded by notification bells, disrupting our focus whenever someone shares something that may or may not be relevant to us. With numerous devices and applications vying for our attention, we squander our most valuable and non-renewable resource: time. Additionally, there is a less obvious loss—our peace of mind.

Our minds are not designed to handle such an overwhelming influx of information. We lack the capacity to process it in a meaningful way. Furthermore, a significant portion of the information we receive is unimportant and merely serves to divert us from the present moment—whether it be delving into the past or future, or becoming engrossed in the lives of others. Neither of these mental distractions contributes to our ability to remain calm.

While using our devices might be important for the daily functioning of our lives, we need to disconnect from them periodically to relax and live mindfully.

*Living mindfully is being aware of what we are feeling at any moment and staying present with whatever is happening.*

Let's say I'm stuck in a traffic jam. Thinking about it isn't going to make the jam go away. I could relax and wait for things to clear up or I could overthink everything that is going to go wrong as a result of it. That will take me into a state of mind that is likely to create all the things I fear.

That does not imply that we don't plan for the future or dip into our experiences to make better decisions. It means that we travel on our timeline just enough to gain from it and no further.

Spending more time in the present moment helps us boost our health and improve our mood. We are able to have better relationships, greater job satisfaction, and good health because it is our inner victories that lead to outer victories, and not the other way around.

# Physical fitness

It is recommended to prioritize at least 30 minutes of physical exercise as part of your daily routine. Engaging in an enjoyable activity such as walking, aerobics, swimming, or yoga can offer numerous benefits for your physical and mental well-being.

Regular physical exercise not only helps maintain your body's fitness but also plays a significant role in reducing anxiety levels. When we exercise, our bodies release endorphins, often referred to as "feel-good hormones." These endorphins contribute to a sense of well-being, uplift our mood, and help alleviate symptoms of anxiety.

Furthermore, physical exercise serves as a healthy outlet for stress and tension. It enables you to redirect your energy toward a productive activity, providing a break from anxious thoughts and worries. The rhythmic movements and increased circulation during exercise also promote relaxation.

Whether it's going for a run, participating in a group exercise class, or swimming laps, find something that brings you joy and fits well with your lifestyle as that will increase your motivation to engage in it consistently.

How many minutes do you exercise in a day?

_______________________________________________

_______________________________________________

_______________________________________________


Are you happy with your exercise regime?

_______________________________________________

_______________________________________________

_______________________________________________


If not, how would you like to change it?

_______________________________________________

_______________________________________________

_______________________________________________


Name three things you can do right away to get started on the new regime?

_______________________________________________

_______________________________________________

_______________________________________________

# Relaxation activities

When we are stressed or anxious it helps to work on our physiology rather than our psychology. Engaging in a relaxing activity that involves our whole body helps soothe our biochemistry and calm our nervous system down. Whenever you feel unsettled, go for a stroll in nature, play a musical instrument, dance, or do something that rejuvenates you. If you can do this for just 10 minutes, you will notice an improvement in your mood.

Tick the activities that you find relaxing:
- Meditation
- Breathing exercises
- Walking in the park
- Aerobics
- Reading
- Dancing
- Playing a musical instrument


Mention any other activities you find relaxing

_______________________________________

_______________________________________

_______________________________________

How many of these activities do you do in a day?

_______________________________________________

_______________________________________________

_______________________________________________

Do you want to increase the time you spend on them? If so, by how much?

_______________________________________________

_______________________________________________

_______________________________________________

Do you want to add any new relaxation exercises to your daily routine?

_______________________________________________

_______________________________________________

_______________________________________________

What can you do to get started on them?

_______________________________________________

_______________________________________________

_______________________________________________

# Focus on the Sounds

Sit comfortably with your eyes closed. Focus on the sounds around you. Is there an air-conditioner on inside your room or birds chirping in the garden? Pay attention to those sounds and be completely present in your environment.

How did you feel before the exercise?

_______________________________________________

_______________________________________________

_______________________________________________

How did you feel after the exercise?

_______________________________________________

_______________________________________________

_______________________________________________

# Your breathing pattern

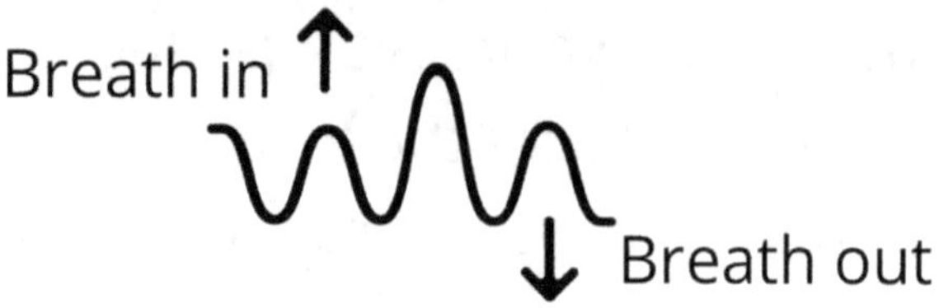


Gently hold your pen between your fingers, positioning it just above the paper. Take a moment to bring your attention to your breath, without attempting to control it. Maintain a relaxed grip on the pen as you begin moving it up and down in its natural rhythm, gliding from the left side to the right side of the page.

While engaging in this activity, keep your focus on your breath—observe the inhalation, the exhalation, and the pauses in between. Rather than adjusting your breath to match the movements of your hand, allow the drawing to naturally reflect your unique breathing pattern.

By directing your attention to your breath and maintaining awareness of its representation on paper, you create less mental space for anxious thoughts to arise.

The pattern that develops through the connection between your breath and the movements of your pen reflects your inner state of mind. If you notice your breathing is shallow and rapid, it indicates you are anxious. Conversely, if your breath is long and spaced out, it indicates a more relaxed state.

# Draw your breathing pattern in the space below

# Focus on your breath

Move your finger along the spiral line, starting from the outer edge and moving toward the center. As you do this, take a deep breath in. Then, breathe out as slowly as you can, following the line outwards. Record your feelings before and after the exercise.

How did you feel before the exercise?

___________________________________

___________________________________

___________________________________

How did you feel after the exercise?

___________________________________

___________________________________

___________________________________

# Progressive relaxation meditation

Let's engage in a simple meditation exercise that will assist in progressively relaxing your mind and body. You can record the following steps as an audio file to create a guided meditation experience on playback.

- Close your eyes.
- Scan your body on the inside from the top of your head down to the tips of your toes. Notice the sensations inside your body.
- Imagine a bright, small ball of light that represents calm
- Place the ball on your ankles and bring your complete awareness to it
- Then move it to your legs, thighs, and hips.
- Then to your upper abdomen (between ribs and belly)
- Chest
- Throat
- Behind the eyebrows
- Above the head
- Make the ball slightly larger and calmer
- Touch the same points on the way down
- Make the ball larger, and go up again
- Do this a few times until you feel completely relaxed.

This progressive relaxation method is most effective when practiced daily—in the morning and before bed. Beginning your day with relaxation helps you approach the challenges ahead with ease. Likewise, engaging in relaxation before sleep promotes a peaceful state of mind throughout the night.

You may have noticed that the last thought before sleep often resurfaces as the first thought upon waking. This is because, during sleep, our conscious mind takes a back seat while our subconscious mind becomes active. The subconscious mind continues to process the information it was last fed, potentially disrupting the quality of our rest.

To optimize the benefits of this practice, it is advisable to avoid checking your phone or engaging with other electronic devices during these crucial hours. Using this time to make to-do lists or dwell on problems can train your mind to be reactive rather than proactive. Instead, claim these hours to connect with the inner silence and derive lasting benefits throughout the day.

# Let's Color

# Monday

DATE:

TODAY I FELT

WHAT WAS ON MY MIND TODAY? HOW DID IT MAKE ME FEEL?

________________________________________________

________________________________________________

________________________________________________

________________________________________________

## WHAT WENT WELL TODAY?

________________________________

________________________________

________________________________

________________________________

________________________________

________________________________

________________________________

## TODAY DID I...

○ SMILE

○ MEDITATE

○ EXERCISE

○ EAT NUTRITIOUS FOOD

○ CATCH FRESH AIR

○ SPEND TIME WITH THE PEOPLE I LOVE

○ SLEEP WELL

## THREE THINGS I AM GRATEFUL FOR

________________________________

________________________________

________________________________

________________________________

________________________________

## I APPRECIATE MYSELF FOR

DID ANYTHING TRIGGER MY ANXIETY TODAY?

_______________________________________________

_______________________________________________

_______________________________________________

_______________________________________________

_______________________________________________

HOW DID I DEAL WITH IT?

_______________________________________________

_______________________________________________

_______________________________________________

_______________________________________________

_______________________________________________

HOW CAN I REFRAME MY ANXIOUS THOUGHTS TO FEEL BETTER?

_______________________________________________

_______________________________________________

_______________________________________________

_______________________________________________

_______________________________________________

THE BEST THING ABOUT TODAY

___________________________

___________________________

___________________________

___________________________

___________________________

___________________________

___________________________

WHAT AM I EXCITED ABOUT FOR TOMORROW?

HOW WELL DID I MANAGE MY ANXIETY TODAY?

☆ ☆ ☆ ☆ ☆

# Tuesday

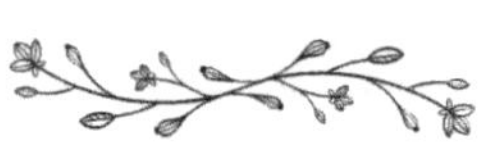

DATE:

TODAY I FELT

WHAT WAS ON MY MIND TODAY? HOW DID IT MAKE ME FEEL?

_______________________________________________

_______________________________________________

_______________________________________________

_______________________________________________

WHAT WENT WELL TODAY?

_____________________________

_____________________________

_____________________________

_____________________________

_____________________________

_____________________________

_____________________________

_____________________________

TODAY DID I...

○ SMILE

○ MEDITATE

○ EXERCISE

○ EAT NUTRITIOUS FOOD

○ CATCH FRESH AIR

○ SPEND TIME WITH THE PEOPLE I LOVE

○ SLEEP WELL

THREE THINGS I AM GRATEFUL FOR

_____________________________

_____________________________

_____________________________

_____________________________

_____________________________

_____________________________

I APPRECIATE MYSELF FOR

DID ANYTHING TRIGGER MY ANXIETY TODAY?

_________________________________________

_________________________________________

_________________________________________

_________________________________________

HOW DID I DEAL WITH IT?

_________________________________________

_________________________________________

_________________________________________

_________________________________________

HOW CAN I REFRAME MY ANXIOUS THOUGHTS TO FEEL BETTER?

_________________________________________

_________________________________________

_________________________________________

_________________________________________

THE BEST THING ABOUT TODAY

WHAT AM I EXCITED ABOUT FOR TOMORROW?

HOW WELL DID I MANAGE MY ANXIETY TODAY?

☆ ☆ ☆ ☆ ☆

# Wednesday

DATE:

TODAY I FELT

## WHAT WAS ON MY MIND TODAY? HOW DID IT MAKE ME FEEL?

## WHAT WENT WELL TODAY?

## TODAY DID I...

- ○ SMILE
- ○ MEDITATE
- ○ EXERCISE
- ○ EAT NUTRITIOUS FOOD
- ○ CATCH FRESH AIR
- ○ SPEND TIME WITH THE PEOPLE I LOVE
- ○ SLEEP WELL

## THREE THINGS I AM GRATEFUL FOR

## I APPRECIATE MYSELF FOR

DID ANYTHING TRIGGER MY ANXIETY TODAY?

HOW DID I DEAL WITH IT?

HOW CAN I REFRAME MY ANXIOUS THOUGHTS TO FEEL BETTER?

THE BEST THING ABOUT TODAY

WHAT AM I EXCITED ABOUT FOR TOMORROW?

HOW WELL DID I MANAGE MY ANXIETY TODAY?

☆ ☆ ☆ ☆ ☆

# Thursday

DATE:

TODAY I FELT

## WHAT WAS ON MY MIND TODAY? HOW DID IT MAKE ME FEEL?

## WHAT WENT WELL TODAY?

## TODAY DID I...

- ○ SMILE
- ○ MEDITATE
- ○ EXERCISE
- ○ EAT NUTRITIOUS FOOD
- ○ CATCH FRESH AIR
- ○ SPEND TIME WITH THE PEOPLE I LOVE
- ○ SLEEP WELL

## THREE THINGS I AM GRATEFUL FOR

## I APPRECIATE MYSELF FOR

DID ANYTHING TRIGGER MY ANXIETY TODAY?

_______________________________________________

_______________________________________________

_______________________________________________

_______________________________________________

HOW DID I DEAL WITH IT?

_______________________________________________

_______________________________________________

_______________________________________________

_______________________________________________

HOW CAN I REFRAME MY ANXIOUS THOUGHTS TO FEEL BETTER?

_______________________________________________

_______________________________________________

_______________________________________________

_______________________________________________

THE BEST THING ABOUT TODAY

___________________________

___________________________

___________________________

___________________________

___________________________

WHAT AM I EXCITED ABOUT FOR TOMORROW?

HOW WELL DID I MANAGE MY ANXIETY TODAY?

☆ ☆ ☆ ☆ ☆

# Friday

DATE:

TODAY I FELT

WHAT WAS ON MY MIND TODAY? HOW DID IT MAKE ME FEEL?

______________________________________________

______________________________________________

______________________________________________

______________________________________________

WHAT WENT WELL TODAY?

____________________________

____________________________

____________________________

____________________________

____________________________

____________________________

____________________________

____________________________

____________________________

TODAY DID I...

○ SMILE

○ MEDITATE

○ EXERCISE

○ EAT NUTRITIOUS FOOD

○ CATCH FRESH AIR

○ SPEND TIME WITH THE PEOPLE I LOVE

○ SLEEP WELL

THREE THINGS I AM GRATEFUL FOR

I APPRECIATE MYSELF FOR

DID ANYTHING TRIGGER MY ANXIETY TODAY?

_______________________________________________

_______________________________________________

_______________________________________________

_______________________________________________

HOW DID I DEAL WITH IT?

_______________________________________________

_______________________________________________

_______________________________________________

_______________________________________________

HOW CAN I REFRAME MY ANXIOUS THOUGHTS TO FEEL BETTER?

_______________________________________________

_______________________________________________

_______________________________________________

_______________________________________________

THE BEST THING ABOUT TODAY

_______________________________

_______________________________

_______________________________

_______________________________

_______________________________

_______________________________

WHAT AM I EXCITED ABOUT FOR TOMORROW?

HOW WELL DID I MANAGE MY ANXIETY TODAY?

☆ ☆ ☆ ☆ ☆

# Saturday

DATE:

TODAY I FELT

## WHAT WAS ON MY MIND TODAY? HOW DID IT MAKE ME FEEL?

## WHAT WENT WELL TODAY?

## TODAY DID I...

- ○ SMILE
- ○ MEDITATE
- ○ EXERCISE
- ○ EAT NUTRITIOUS FOOD
- ○ CATCH FRESH AIR
- ○ SPEND TIME WITH THE PEOPLE I LOVE
- ○ SLEEP WELL

## THREE THINGS I AM GRATEFUL FOR

## I APPRECIATE MYSELF FOR

DID ANYTHING TRIGGER MY ANXIETY TODAY?

_______________________________________________

_______________________________________________

_______________________________________________

_______________________________________________

_______________________________________________

HOW DID I DEAL WITH IT?

_______________________________________________

_______________________________________________

_______________________________________________

_______________________________________________

_______________________________________________

HOW CAN I REFRAME MY ANXIOUS THOUGHTS TO FEEL BETTER?

_______________________________________________

_______________________________________________

_______________________________________________

_______________________________________________

_______________________________________________

THE BEST THING ABOUT TODAY

WHAT AM I EXCITED ABOUT FOR TOMORROW?

HOW WELL DID I MANAGE MY ANXIETY TODAY?

☆ ☆ ☆ ☆ ☆

# Sunday

**DATE:**

**TODAY I FELT**

**WHAT WAS ON MY MIND TODAY? HOW DID IT MAKE ME FEEL?**

________________________________________

________________________________________

________________________________________

________________________________________

**WHAT WENT WELL TODAY?**

________________________________________

________________________________________

________________________________________

________________________________________

________________________________________

________________________________________

________________________________________

**TODAY DID I...**

○ SMILE

○ MEDITATE

○ EXERCISE

○ EAT NUTRITIOUS FOOD

○ CATCH FRESH AIR

○ SPEND TIME WITH THE PEOPLE I LOVE

○ SLEEP WELL

**THREE THINGS I AM GRATEFUL FOR**

________________________________________

________________________________________

________________________________________

________________________________________

**I APPRECIATE MYSELF FOR**

DID ANYTHING TRIGGER MY ANXIETY TODAY?

HOW DID I DEAL WITH IT?

HOW CAN I REFRAME MY ANXIOUS THOUGHTS TO FEEL BETTER?

THE BEST THING ABOUT TODAY

WHAT AM I EXCITED ABOUT FOR TOMORROW?

HOW WELL DID I MANAGE MY ANXIETY TODAY?

☆ ☆ ☆ ☆ ☆

# Week 5
# Check in

DATE:

WHAT DID I DO WELL THIS WEEK?

_______________________________

_______________________________

_______________________________

_______________________________

THIS WEEK I FELT

HOW WELL DID I MANAGE MY ANXIETY THIS WEEK?

WHAT DID I DO WELL THIS WEEK?

_______________________________

_______________________________

_______________________________

_______________________________

WHAT WOULD I LIKE TO DO BETTER NEXT WEEK?

WHAT AM I EXCITED ABOUT IN THE UPCOMING WEEK?

# The Fear of Past Events

IT'S OKAY TO BE SCARED.
BEING SCARED MEANS YOU
ARE ABOUT TO DO
SOMETHING REALLY BRAVE.
– MANDY HALE

# The Fear of Past Events

Anxiety requires us to be skilled at imagination. When we are anxious, we often imagine worst-case scenarios that haven't happened yet. Over time, this creates circuits in our brains that are easily triggered even by weak stimuli.

You might remember a time, perhaps when you were a kid, when you found it difficult to feel anxious about anything for more than a few minutes. You quickly got bored of the feeling or got distracted by something more interesting. However, over time, the ability to snap out of anxiety diminished.

This typically happens when you practice feeling anxious over and over again until it is no longer a habit; it becomes expert behavior. The neural pathways grow stronger with every moment spent being anxious until it becomes easier to slip into that state.

Previously, you might have only felt anxious about giving an important presentation, but now, if someone just says they want to speak with you, it might be sufficient to trigger anxiety.

*Practice what you want because practice makes perfect!*

# The self-fulfilling prophecy

Our bad experiences put us on high alert. We often feel scared of the same event happening again and behave in ways to avoid it. This constant focus on ensuring that the painful event doesn't recur can take us away from the present moment.

Repetitively recalling a painful memory strengthens the associated neural pathway and increases the likelihood of encountering similar situations in the future. This is known as a self-fulfilling prophecy—what we try to avoid, we end up attracting.

Let's say you want to be friends with someone, but you can't stop thinking about the time they hurt you. Having that memory constantly at the forefront of your mind might cause you to unconsciously behave in ways that push the person away, despite consciously believing that you are doing your best to build the relationship.

# Calm Your Worries

Are you worried about a future event? Whenever you catch yourself drifting into visualizing unwanted scenarios, write an entry in the table.

| Today's Date | What am I worried about? | Date by which I expect this to happen | Did it happen? |
|---|---|---|---|
| | | | |

Fill in the fields in the table, except for the last column. After the date by which you expected the event to happen, fill in the last column, mentioning whether the event occurred or not. Over time, this table will give you an estimate of the energy spent worrying about things that never happened. Every time you write an entry, you will start to challenge the likelihood of your worries coming true.

Affirm to yourself, "Whatever happened in the past is over. I might not have had the strength to deal with that situation then, but today things are different. I can deal with it very well if I had to. My experiences have made me powerful enough to do so."

## Positive Visualization

Visualization can be a powerful tool to transform your mindset. When we are anxious, we use it to create stressful scenarios that can affect us adversely. However, when it is used to create a nurturing environment inside our minds, it can be the most powerful tool in our arsenal. Regardless of what is happening outside, we can be happy and satisfied on the inside.

Whenever you experience anxiety, try visualizing your worries as leaves floating away in a stream of water. Imagine them being carried away by the stream, gradually fading from sight, until they vanish completely.

If you have a particular fear, such as speaking to a specific person, engage in positive visualization. Frequently picture yourself confidently talking to that person. Notice yourself enjoying the process. When you meet that person next, you will be able to face him/her confidently.

By repeatedly envisioning yourself successfully overcoming your fears, you create neural pathways that promote the occurrence of that event. The more you practice and succeed in overcoming anxiety through your visualizations, the more it will translate into increased confidence in facing those challenges.

#  Monday

DATE:

TODAY I FELT

## WHAT WAS ON MY MIND TODAY? HOW DID IT MAKE ME FEEL?

_______________________________________________

_______________________________________________

_______________________________________________

_______________________________________________

## WHAT WENT WELL TODAY?

_____________________________________

_____________________________________

_____________________________________

_____________________________________

_____________________________________

_____________________________________

_____________________________________

_____________________________________

## TODAY DID I...

○ SMILE

○ MEDITATE

○ EXERCISE

○ EAT NUTRITIOUS FOOD

○ CATCH FRESH AIR

○ SPEND TIME WITH THE PEOPLE I LOVE

○ SLEEP WELL

## THREE THINGS I AM GRATEFUL FOR

_____________________________________

_____________________________________

_____________________________________

_____________________________________

_____________________________________

_____________________________________

## I APPRECIATE MYSELF FOR

DID ANYTHING TRIGGER MY ANXIETY TODAY?

_______________________________________________

_______________________________________________

_______________________________________________

_______________________________________________

_______________________________________________

HOW DID I DEAL WITH IT?

_______________________________________________

_______________________________________________

_______________________________________________

_______________________________________________

_______________________________________________

HOW CAN I REFRAME MY ANXIOUS THOUGHTS TO FEEL BETTER?

_______________________________________________

_______________________________________________

_______________________________________________

_______________________________________________

_______________________________________________

THE BEST THING ABOUT TODAY

_______________________________

_______________________________

_______________________________

_______________________________

_______________________________

_______________________________

_______________________________

WHAT AM I EXCITED ABOUT FOR TOMORROW?

HOW WELL DID I MANAGE MY ANXIETY TODAY?

☆ ☆ ☆ ☆ ☆

# Tuesday

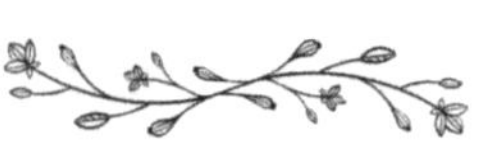

DATE:

TODAY I FELT

## WHAT WAS ON MY MIND TODAY? HOW DID IT MAKE ME FEEL?

_______________________________________________

_______________________________________________

_______________________________________________

_______________________________________________

## WHAT WENT WELL TODAY?

______________________________

______________________________

______________________________

______________________________

______________________________

______________________________

______________________________

______________________________

## TODAY DID I...

- ○ SMILE
- ○ MEDITATE
- ○ EXERCISE
- ○ EAT NUTRITIOUS FOOD
- ○ CATCH FRESH AIR
- ○ SPEND TIME WITH THE PEOPLE I LOVE
- ○ SLEEP WELL

## THREE THINGS I AM GRATEFUL FOR

______________________________

______________________________

______________________________

______________________________

______________________________

______________________________

## I APPRECIATE MYSELF FOR

DID ANYTHING TRIGGER MY ANXIETY TODAY?

_______________________________________

_______________________________________

_______________________________________

_______________________________________

HOW DID I DEAL WITH IT?

_______________________________________

_______________________________________

_______________________________________

_______________________________________

HOW CAN I REFRAME MY ANXIOUS THOUGHTS TO FEEL BETTER?

_______________________________________

_______________________________________

_______________________________________

_______________________________________

THE BEST THING ABOUT TODAY

_______________________

_______________________

_______________________

_______________________

_______________________

_______________________

WHAT AM I EXCITED ABOUT FOR TOMORROW?

HOW WELL DID I MANAGE MY ANXIETY TODAY?

☆ ☆ ☆ ☆ ☆

# Wednesday

DATE:

TODAY I FELT

WHAT WAS ON MY MIND TODAY? HOW DID IT MAKE ME FEEL?

_______________________________________________

_______________________________________________

_______________________________________________

_______________________________________________

_______________________________________________

## WHAT WENT WELL TODAY?

_________________________________

_________________________________

_________________________________

_________________________________

_________________________________

_________________________________

_________________________________

_________________________________

## TODAY DID I...

- ○ SMILE
- ○ MEDITATE
- ○ EXERCISE
- ○ EAT NUTRITIOUS FOOD
- ○ CATCH FRESH AIR
- ○ SPEND TIME WITH THE PEOPLE I LOVE
- ○ SLEEP WELL

## THREE THINGS I AM GRATEFUL FOR

_________________________________

_________________________________

_________________________________

_________________________________

_________________________________

## I APPRECIATE MYSELF FOR

DID ANYTHING TRIGGER MY ANXIETY TODAY?

HOW DID I DEAL WITH IT?

HOW CAN I REFRAME MY ANXIOUS THOUGHTS TO FEEL BETTER?

THE BEST THING ABOUT TODAY

WHAT AM I EXCITED ABOUT FOR TOMORROW?

HOW WELL DID I MANAGE MY ANXIETY TODAY?

☆ ☆ ☆ ☆ ☆

# Thursday

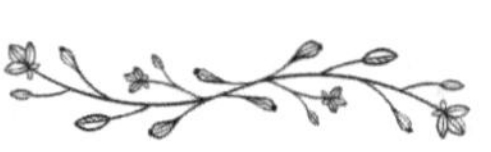

DATE:

TODAY I FELT

WHAT WAS ON MY MIND TODAY? HOW DID IT MAKE ME FEEL?

WHAT WENT WELL TODAY?

TODAY DID I...

- ○ SMILE
- ○ MEDITATE
- ○ EXERCISE
- ○ EAT NUTRITIOUS FOOD
- ○ CATCH FRESH AIR
- ○ SPEND TIME WITH THE PEOPLE I LOVE
- ○ SLEEP WELL

THREE THINGS I AM GRATEFUL FOR

I APPRECIATE MYSELF FOR

DID ANYTHING TRIGGER MY ANXIETY TODAY?

_______________________________________________

_______________________________________________

_______________________________________________

_______________________________________________

HOW DID I DEAL WITH IT?

_______________________________________________

_______________________________________________

_______________________________________________

_______________________________________________

HOW CAN I REFRAME MY ANXIOUS THOUGHTS TO FEEL BETTER?

_______________________________________________

_______________________________________________

_______________________________________________

_______________________________________________

THE BEST THING ABOUT TODAY

_______________________________

_______________________________

_______________________________

_______________________________

_______________________________

_______________________________

WHAT AM I EXCITED ABOUT FOR TOMORROW?

HOW WELL DID I MANAGE MY ANXIETY TODAY?

☆ ☆ ☆ ☆ ☆

# *Friday*

DATE:

TODAY I FELT
_______________________

WHAT WAS ON MY MIND TODAY? HOW DID IT MAKE ME FEEL?

_______________________________________________
_______________________________________________
_______________________________________________
_______________________________________________

WHAT WENT WELL TODAY?

_______________________________
_______________________________
_______________________________
_______________________________
_______________________________
_______________________________
_______________________________
_______________________________

TODAY DID I...

○ SMILE

○ MEDITATE

○ EXERCISE

○ EAT NUTRITIOUS FOOD

○ CATCH FRESH AIR

○ SPEND TIME WITH THE PEOPLE I LOVE

○ SLEEP WELL

THREE THINGS I AM GRATEFUL FOR

_______________________________
_______________________________
_______________________________
_______________________________
_______________________________
_______________________________

I APPRECIATE MYSELF FOR

DID ANYTHING TRIGGER MY ANXIETY TODAY?

_______________________________________________

_______________________________________________

_______________________________________________

_______________________________________________

HOW DID I DEAL WITH IT?

_______________________________________________

_______________________________________________

_______________________________________________

_______________________________________________

HOW CAN I REFRAME MY ANXIOUS THOUGHTS TO FEEL BETTER?

_______________________________________________

_______________________________________________

_______________________________________________

_______________________________________________

THE BEST THING ABOUT TODAY

_______________________________

_______________________________

_______________________________

_______________________________

_______________________________

_______________________________

WHAT AM I EXCITED ABOUT FOR TOMORROW?

HOW WELL DID I MANAGE MY ANXIETY TODAY?

☆ ☆ ☆ ☆ ☆

# *Saturday*

DATE:

TODAY I FELT

## WHAT WAS ON MY MIND TODAY? HOW DID IT MAKE ME FEEL?

___________________________________________

___________________________________________

___________________________________________

___________________________________________

## WHAT WENT WELL TODAY?

_________________________________

_________________________________

_________________________________

_________________________________

_________________________________

_________________________________

_________________________________

_________________________________

## TODAY DID I...

○ SMILE

○ MEDITATE

○ EXERCISE

○ EAT NUTRITIOUS FOOD

○ CATCH FRESH AIR

○ SPEND TIME WITH THE PEOPLE I LOVE

○ SLEEP WELL

## THREE THINGS I AM GRATEFUL FOR

_________________________________

_________________________________

_________________________________

_________________________________

_________________________________

_________________________________

## I APPRECIATE MYSELF FOR

DID ANYTHING TRIGGER MY ANXIETY TODAY?

HOW DID I DEAL WITH IT?

HOW CAN I REFRAME MY ANXIOUS THOUGHTS TO FEEL BETTER?

THE BEST THING ABOUT TODAY

WHAT AM I EXCITED ABOUT FOR TOMORROW?

HOW WELL DID I MANAGE MY ANXIETY TODAY?

☆ ☆ ☆ ☆ ☆

# Sunday

DATE:

TODAY I FELT

WHAT WAS ON MY MIND TODAY? HOW DID IT MAKE ME FEEL?

______________________________________________

______________________________________________

______________________________________________

______________________________________________

______________________________________________

## WHAT WENT WELL TODAY?

__________________________________

__________________________________

__________________________________

__________________________________

__________________________________

__________________________________

__________________________________

__________________________________

## TODAY DID I...

- ○ SMILE
- ○ MEDITATE
- ○ EXERCISE
- ○ EAT NUTRITIOUS FOOD
- ○ CATCH FRESH AIR
- ○ SPEND TIME WITH THE PEOPLE I LOVE
- ○ SLEEP WELL

## THREE THINGS I AM GRATEFUL FOR

__________________________________

__________________________________

__________________________________

__________________________________

__________________________________

__________________________________

## I APPRECIATE MYSELF FOR

## DID ANYTHING TRIGGER MY ANXIETY TODAY?

## HOW DID I DEAL WITH IT?

## HOW CAN I REFRAME MY ANXIOUS THOUGHTS TO FEEL BETTER?

## THE BEST THING ABOUT TODAY

## WHAT AM I EXCITED ABOUT FOR TOMORROW?

## HOW WELL DID I MANAGE MY ANXIETY TODAY?

☆ ☆ ☆ ☆ ☆

# Week 6
# Check in

## WHAT DID I DO WELL THIS WEEK?

_______________________________________________

_______________________________________________

_______________________________________________

_______________________________________________

## THIS WEEK I FELT

## HOW WELL DID I MANAGE MY ANXIETY THIS WEEK?

☆ ☆ ☆ ☆ ☆

## WHAT DID I DO WELL THIS WEEK?

_______________________________________________

_______________________________________________

_______________________________________________

_______________________________________________

## WHAT WOULD I LIKE TO DO BETTER NEXT WEEK?

## WHAT AM I EXCITED ABOUT IN THE UPCOMING WEEK?

# Breaking into Baby Steps

> WHATEVER YOU IMAGINE ALREADY EXISTS IN THE DIMENSION OF YOUR MIND
> – DR. JOSEPH MURPHY

# Breaking into Baby Steps

If you find yourself anxious about an upcoming event where the workload feels daunting, here is a strategy you can employ to alleviate your anxiety. Break the task down into baby steps. Each step should feel safe—one you can visualize yourself doing. Execute the first step in this list. Since you have attempted a step that feels safe to you, the chances of your going through with it will be high. For instance, you have an elaborate document that you need to complete in four days. You are overwhelmed as it needs too much work to be done in very little time. Start with breaking down the document into sections. Create intermediate milestones—ones you can see yourself achieving. Focus only on completing the first section. The momentum will help you complete the other sections as well.

*Motivation is not only the cause of action, it is the result of it too.*

The anxiety about doing the big task gets replaced with the momentum of completing it. As you approach completion, you will observe a surge in your pace due to the growing clarity with which you can envision your result.

# Breaking into Baby Steps

If you find yourself anxious about an upcoming event where the workload feels daunting, here is a strategy you can employ to alleviate your anxiety. Break the task into baby steps. Each step should feel safe—one you can visualize yourself doing.

Execute the first step in this list. Since you have attempted a step that feels safe to you, the chances of your going through with it will be high. For instance, you have an elaborate document that you need to complete in four days. You are overwhelmed as it needs too much work to be done in very little time. Start with breaking down the document into sections. Create intermediate milestones—ones you can see yourself achieving. Focus only on completing the first section. The momentum will help you complete the other sections as well.

*Motivation is not only the cause of action, it is the result of it too.*

The anxiety about doing a big task gets replaced with the momentum of completing it. As you approach completion, you will observe a surge in your pace due to the growing clarity with which you can envision your result.

# Too many tasks?

If you are stressed about having too many tasks that need to be done at once, list them down. Prioritize them based on their importance and desired date of completion. Start with a task that is important and relatively easy to do.

List your tasks starting with the greatest priority down to the lowest one.

_______________________________________

_______________________________________

_______________________________________

_______________________________________

_______________________________________

_______________________________________

Can you start with the first task on your list?

_______________________________________

Can you visualize yourself doing it?

_______________________________________

(If it is overwhelming, break it down into steps, as suggested in the previous exercise.)

# Make your task list

☐ _______________________

☐ _______________________

☐ _______________________

☐ _______________________

☐ _______________________

☐ _______________________

☐ _______________________

☐ _______________________

**Pro Tip**

As soon as you complete a task, check it off your list. The satisfaction you feel from ticking off tasks will propel you forward. You might even accomplish more than you initially set out to do.

# Let's Color

DATE:

TODAY I FELT

WHAT WAS ON MY MIND TODAY? HOW DID IT MAKE ME FEEL?

_______________________________________________

_______________________________________________

_______________________________________________

_______________________________________________

WHAT WENT WELL TODAY?

_______________________________

_______________________________

_______________________________

_______________________________

_______________________________

_______________________________

_______________________________

_______________________________

TODAY DID I...

○ SMILE

○ MEDITATE

○ EXERCISE

○ EAT NUTRITIOUS FOOD

○ CATCH FRESH AIR

○ SPEND TIME WITH THE PEOPLE I LOVE

○ SLEEP WELL

THREE THINGS I AM GRATEFUL FOR

_______________________________

_______________________________

_______________________________

_______________________________

I APPRECIATE MYSELF FOR

DID ANYTHING TRIGGER MY ANXIETY TODAY?

________________________________________

________________________________________

________________________________________

________________________________________

HOW DID I DEAL WITH IT?

________________________________________

________________________________________

________________________________________

________________________________________

HOW CAN I REFRAME MY ANXIOUS THOUGHTS TO FEEL BETTER?

________________________________________

________________________________________

________________________________________

________________________________________

THE BEST THING ABOUT TODAY

________________________________

________________________________

________________________________

________________________________

________________________________

________________________________

WHAT AM I EXCITED ABOUT FOR TOMORROW?

HOW WELL DID I MANAGE MY ANXIETY TODAY?

☆ ☆ ☆ ☆ ☆

# Tuesday

DATE:

TODAY I FELT

## WHAT WAS ON MY MIND TODAY? HOW DID IT MAKE ME FEEL?

_______________________________________________

_______________________________________________

_______________________________________________

_______________________________________________

_______________________________________________

## WHAT WENT WELL TODAY?

_________________________________

_________________________________

_________________________________

_________________________________

_________________________________

_________________________________

_________________________________

_________________________________

## TODAY DID I...

○ SMILE

○ MEDITATE

○ EXERCISE

○ EAT NUTRITIOUS FOOD

○ CATCH FRESH AIR

○ SPEND TIME WITH THE
   PEOPLE I LOVE

○ SLEEP WELL

## THREE THINGS I AM GRATEFUL FOR

_________________________________

_________________________________

_________________________________

_________________________________

_________________________________

## I APPRECIATE MYSELF FOR

DID ANYTHING TRIGGER MY ANXIETY TODAY?

____________________________________________

____________________________________________

____________________________________________

____________________________________________

HOW DID I DEAL WITH IT?

____________________________________________

____________________________________________

____________________________________________

____________________________________________

HOW CAN I REFRAME MY ANXIOUS THOUGHTS TO FEEL BETTER?

____________________________________________

____________________________________________

____________________________________________

____________________________________________

THE BEST THING ABOUT TODAY

__________________________

__________________________

__________________________

__________________________

__________________________

__________________________

WHAT AM I EXCITED ABOUT FOR TOMORROW?



HOW WELL DID I MANAGE MY ANXIETY TODAY?

☆ ☆ ☆ ☆ ☆

# Wednesday

DATE:

TODAY I FELT
___________________________

WHAT WAS ON MY MIND TODAY? HOW DID IT MAKE ME FEEL?

_______________________________________________

_______________________________________________

_______________________________________________

_______________________________________________

_______________________________________________

## WHAT WENT WELL TODAY?

_________________________________

_________________________________

_________________________________

_________________________________

_________________________________

_________________________________

_________________________________

_________________________________

_________________________________

## TODAY DID I...

- ○ SMILE
- ○ MEDITATE
- ○ EXERCISE
- ○ EAT NUTRITIOUS FOOD
- ○ CATCH FRESH AIR
- ○ SPEND TIME WITH THE PEOPLE I LOVE
- ○ SLEEP WELL

## THREE THINGS I AM GRATEFUL FOR

_________________________________

_________________________________

_________________________________

_________________________________

_________________________________

_________________________________

## I APPRECIATE MYSELF FOR

DID ANYTHING TRIGGER MY ANXIETY TODAY?

HOW DID I DEAL WITH IT?

HOW CAN I REFRAME MY ANXIOUS THOUGHTS TO FEEL BETTER?

THE BEST THING ABOUT TODAY

WHAT AM I EXCITED ABOUT FOR TOMORROW?

HOW WELL DID I MANAGE MY ANXIETY TODAY?
☆ ☆ ☆ ☆ ☆

DATE:

TODAY I FELT

WHAT WAS ON MY MIND TODAY? HOW DID IT MAKE ME FEEL?

___________________________________________

___________________________________________

___________________________________________

___________________________________________

___________________________________________

WHAT WENT WELL TODAY?

___________________________________

___________________________________

___________________________________

___________________________________

___________________________________

___________________________________

___________________________________

___________________________________

TODAY DID I...

○ SMILE

○ MEDITATE

○ EXERCISE

○ EAT NUTRITIOUS FOOD

○ CATCH FRESH AIR

○ SPEND TIME WITH THE PEOPLE I LOVE

○ SLEEP WELL

THREE THINGS I AM GRATEFUL FOR

___________________________________

___________________________________

___________________________________

___________________________________

___________________________________

I APPRECIATE MYSELF FOR

DID ANYTHING TRIGGER MY ANXIETY TODAY?

_______________________________________________
_______________________________________________
_______________________________________________
_______________________________________________
_______________________________________________

HOW DID I DEAL WITH IT?

_______________________________________________
_______________________________________________
_______________________________________________
_______________________________________________
_______________________________________________

HOW CAN I REFRAME MY ANXIOUS THOUGHTS TO FEEL BETTER?

_______________________________________________
_______________________________________________
_______________________________________________
_______________________________________________
_______________________________________________

THE BEST THING ABOUT TODAY

______________________________
______________________________
______________________________
______________________________
______________________________
______________________________

WHAT AM I EXCITED ABOUT FOR TOMORROW?




HOW WELL DID I MANAGE MY ANXIETY TODAY?

☆ ☆ ☆ ☆ ☆

# Friday

DATE:

TODAY I FELT

WHAT WAS ON MY MIND TODAY? HOW DID IT MAKE ME FEEL?

___________________________________________

___________________________________________

___________________________________________

___________________________________________

WHAT WENT WELL TODAY?

_______________________________

_______________________________

_______________________________

_______________________________

_______________________________

_______________________________

_______________________________

_______________________________

TODAY DID I...

○ SMILE

○ MEDITATE

○ EXERCISE

○ EAT NUTRITIOUS FOOD

○ CATCH FRESH AIR

○ SPEND TIME WITH THE PEOPLE I LOVE

○ SLEEP WELL

THREE THINGS I AM GRATEFUL FOR

_______________________________

_______________________________

_______________________________

_______________________________

I APPRECIATE MYSELF FOR

DID ANYTHING TRIGGER MY ANXIETY TODAY?

_______________________________________________

_______________________________________________

_______________________________________________

_______________________________________________

HOW DID I DEAL WITH IT?

_______________________________________________

_______________________________________________

_______________________________________________

_______________________________________________

HOW CAN I REFRAME MY ANXIOUS THOUGHTS TO FEEL BETTER?

_______________________________________________

_______________________________________________

_______________________________________________

_______________________________________________

THE BEST THING ABOUT TODAY

_________________________________

_________________________________

_________________________________

_________________________________

_________________________________

_________________________________

WHAT AM I EXCITED ABOUT FOR TOMORROW?

HOW WELL DID I MANAGE MY ANXIETY TODAY?

☆ ☆ ☆ ☆ ☆

# Saturday

DATE:

TODAY I FELT
________________________

## WHAT WAS ON MY MIND TODAY? HOW DID IT MAKE ME FEEL?

__________________________________________

__________________________________________

__________________________________________

__________________________________________

__________________________________________

## WHAT WENT WELL TODAY?

______________________________

______________________________

______________________________

______________________________

______________________________

______________________________

______________________________

______________________________

## TODAY DID I...

- ○ SMILE
- ○ MEDITATE
- ○ EXERCISE
- ○ EAT NUTRITIOUS FOOD
- ○ CATCH FRESH AIR
- ○ SPEND TIME WITH THE PEOPLE I LOVE
- ○ SLEEP WELL

## THREE THINGS I AM GRATEFUL FOR

______________________________

______________________________

______________________________

______________________________

______________________________

## I APPRECIATE MYSELF FOR

DID ANYTHING TRIGGER MY ANXIETY TODAY?

HOW DID I DEAL WITH IT?

HOW CAN I REFRAME MY ANXIOUS THOUGHTS TO FEEL BETTER?

THE BEST THING ABOUT TODAY

WHAT AM I EXCITED ABOUT FOR TOMORROW?

HOW WELL DID I MANAGE MY ANXIETY TODAY?

☆ ☆ ☆ ☆ ☆

DATE:

TODAY I FELT

## WHAT WAS ON MY MIND TODAY? HOW DID IT MAKE ME FEEL?

## WHAT WENT WELL TODAY?

## TODAY DID I...

○ SMILE

○ MEDITATE

○ EXERCISE

○ EAT NUTRITIOUS FOOD

○ CATCH FRESH AIR

○ SPEND TIME WITH THE PEOPLE I LOVE

○ SLEEP WELL

## THREE THINGS I AM GRATEFUL FOR

## I APPRECIATE MYSELF FOR

DID ANYTHING TRIGGER MY ANXIETY TODAY?

HOW DID I DEAL WITH IT?

HOW CAN I REFRAME MY ANXIOUS THOUGHTS TO FEEL BETTER?

THE BEST THING ABOUT TODAY

WHAT AM I EXCITED ABOUT FOR TOMORROW?

HOW WELL DID I MANAGE MY ANXIETY TODAY?

☆ ☆ ☆ ☆ ☆

# Week 7 Check in



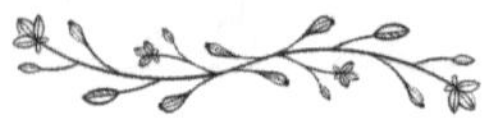

## WHAT DID I DO WELL THIS WEEK?

________________________________________

________________________________________

________________________________________

________________________________________

## THIS WEEK I FELT

## HOW WELL DID I MANAGE MY ANXIETY THIS WEEK?

## WHAT DID I DO WELL THIS WEEK?

________________________________________

________________________________________

________________________________________

________________________________________

## WHAT WOULD I LIKE TO DO BETTER NEXT WEEK?

## WHAT AM I EXCITED ABOUT IN THE UPCOMING WEEK?

# Your Resources

"

AS YOU THINK THOUGHTS
THAT FEEL GOOD TO YOU,
YOU WILL BE IN HARMONY
WITH WHO YOU REALLY ARE

– ABRAHAM HICKS

# Your Resources

We have two primary resources that support us in our endeavors:

1) Internal Resources: These are the assets that reside within us, such as confidence, motivation, hard work, willpower, and other personal qualities.

2) External Resources: These encompass the resources that exist outside of us, such as mentors, financial support, training opportunities, and other external factors that contribute to our success.

## Internal resources

By identifying the capabilities required for a certain task and actively working on developing our skills, we can reduce the anxiety associated with it. We can enhance our internal resources by building our physical and mental endurance and cultivating good habits that promote focus. By doing so, we strengthen our internal foundation, leading to more confidence and less anxiety.

*One way to be more confident is to be more competent*

# Identify your internal resources

What are your top accomplishments?

_______________________________________

_______________________________________

_______________________________________

What strengths did you use to achieve them?

_______________________________________

_______________________________________

_______________________________________

What is your greatest weakness?

_______________________________________

_______________________________________

_______________________________________

What is the strength that is hidden in it?

_______________________________________

_______________________________________

# External resources

Imagine a person residing within a system consisting of three other individuals, such as a family or a group of roommates. Whenever one person encounters a problem, the other three promptly support him/her. In such a system, the anxiety levels of each person would be lower, as there is a sense of collective support and care.

On the contrary, if a person resides in a hostile environment where individuals within the system cannot be relied upon to stand up for each other, it can aggravate feelings of anxiety.

The presence or absence of a reliable support system has a profound impact on our overall well-being. Hence, to reduce our anxiety it helps to nurture deep, meaningful relationships with people who are important to us.

# Resource check

Think of a challenge you faced sometime in life.

What internal resources helped you come out of it (motivation, willpower, hard work, commitment, dedication, etc.)?

___________________________________________

___________________________________________

___________________________________________

Do you have these internal resources today as well?

______________________________________

______________________________________

______________________________________

If you were to face a difficult situation in the future, what external resources (people, time, money, training, etc.) would you have at your disposal?

______________________________________

______________________________________

______________________________________

If you don't have these internal or external resources today, what can you do to nurture them so that they can be available to support you tomorrow?

______________________________________

______________________________________

______________________________________

# Your pillars of strength

On each pillar below, write the name of a person you consider as your pillar of strength. Visualize them and their qualities: What do you like about them? How do they treat you?

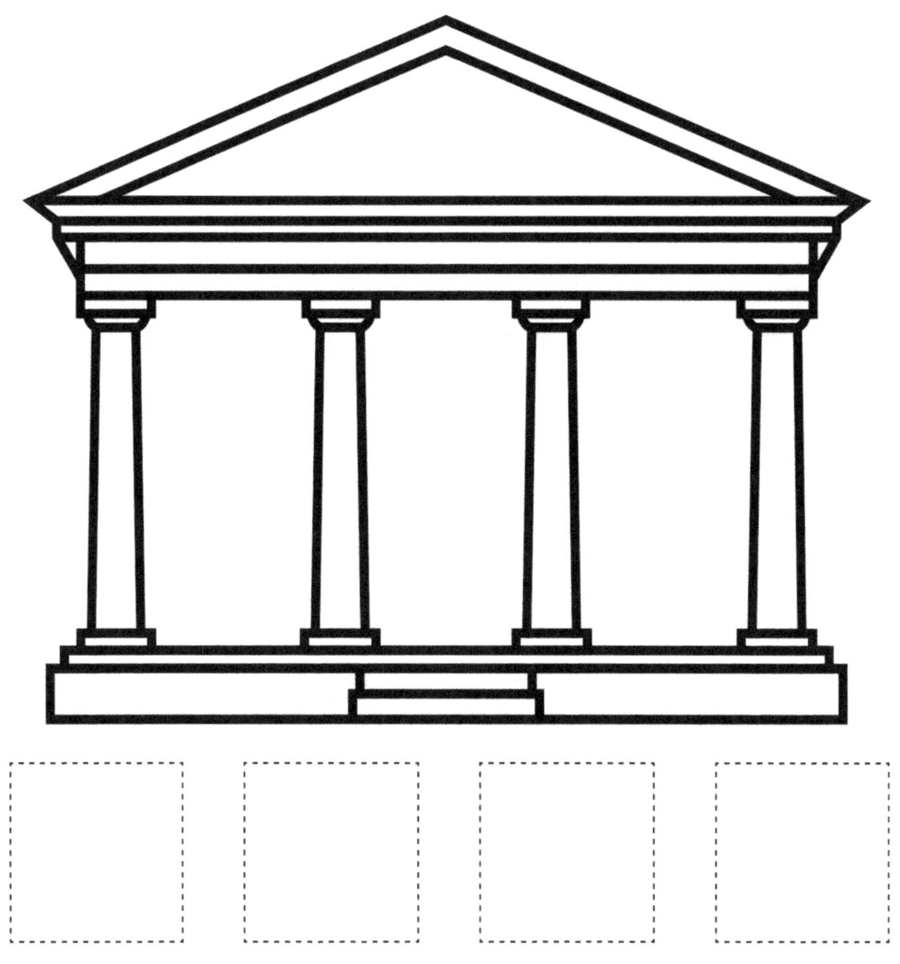

Extend your gratitude. Draw a gift for each of them in the boxes above.

# Monday

DATE:

TODAY I FELT
________________________

WHAT WAS ON MY MIND TODAY? HOW DID IT MAKE ME FEEL?

______________________________

______________________________

______________________________

______________________________

______________________________

## WHAT WENT WELL TODAY?

______________________________

______________________________

______________________________

______________________________

______________________________

______________________________

______________________________

______________________________

______________________________

## TODAY DID I...

○ SMILE

○ MEDITATE

○ EXERCISE

○ EAT NUTRITIOUS FOOD

○ CATCH FRESH AIR

○ SPEND TIME WITH THE PEOPLE I LOVE

○ SLEEP WELL

## THREE THINGS I AM GRATEFUL FOR

______________________________

______________________________

______________________________

______________________________

______________________________

## I APPRECIATE MYSELF FOR

DID ANYTHING TRIGGER MY ANXIETY TODAY?

HOW DID I DEAL WITH IT?

HOW CAN I REFRAME MY ANXIOUS THOUGHTS TO FEEL BETTER?

THE BEST THING ABOUT TODAY

WHAT AM I EXCITED ABOUT FOR TOMORROW?

HOW WELL DID I MANAGE MY ANXIETY TODAY?
☆ ☆ ☆ ☆ ☆

# Tuesday

DATE:

TODAY I FELT

WHAT WAS ON MY MIND TODAY? HOW DID IT MAKE ME FEEL?

___________________________________________

___________________________________________

___________________________________________

___________________________________________

WHAT WENT WELL TODAY?

_______________________________

_______________________________

_______________________________

_______________________________

_______________________________

_______________________________

_______________________________

_______________________________

TODAY DID I...

○ SMILE

○ MEDITATE

○ EXERCISE

○ EAT NUTRITIOUS FOOD

○ CATCH FRESH AIR

○ SPEND TIME WITH THE PEOPLE I LOVE

○ SLEEP WELL

THREE THINGS I AM GRATEFUL FOR

_______________________________

_______________________________

_______________________________

_______________________________

_______________________________

_______________________________

I APPRECIATE MYSELF FOR

DID ANYTHING TRIGGER MY ANXIETY TODAY?

HOW DID I DEAL WITH IT?

HOW CAN I REFRAME MY ANXIOUS THOUGHTS TO FEEL BETTER?

THE BEST THING ABOUT TODAY

WHAT AM I EXCITED ABOUT FOR TOMORROW?

HOW WELL DID I MANAGE MY ANXIETY TODAY?

☆ ☆ ☆ ☆ ☆

# Wednesday

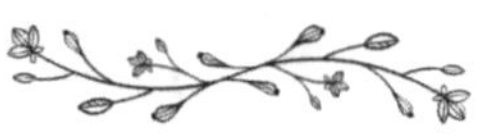

DATE:

TODAY I FELT

WHAT WAS ON MY MIND TODAY? HOW DID IT MAKE ME FEEL?

_______________________________________________

_______________________________________________

_______________________________________________

_______________________________________________

WHAT WENT WELL TODAY?

_____________________________

_____________________________

_____________________________

_____________________________

_____________________________

_____________________________

_____________________________

_____________________________

TODAY DID I...

○ SMILE

○ MEDITATE

○ EXERCISE

○ EAT NUTRITIOUS FOOD

○ CATCH FRESH AIR

○ SPEND TIME WITH THE PEOPLE I LOVE

○ SLEEP WELL

THREE THINGS I AM GRATEFUL FOR

_____________________________

_____________________________

_____________________________

_____________________________

_____________________________

_____________________________

I APPRECIATE MYSELF FOR

DID ANYTHING TRIGGER MY ANXIETY TODAY?

_______________________________________________

_______________________________________________

_______________________________________________

_______________________________________________

HOW DID I DEAL WITH IT?

_______________________________________________

_______________________________________________

_______________________________________________

_______________________________________________

HOW CAN I REFRAME MY ANXIOUS THOUGHTS TO FEEL BETTER?

_______________________________________________

_______________________________________________

_______________________________________________

_______________________________________________

THE BEST THING ABOUT TODAY

_______________________________

_______________________________

_______________________________

_______________________________

_______________________________

_______________________________

WHAT AM I EXCITED ABOUT FOR TOMORROW?

HOW WELL DID I MANAGE MY ANXIETY TODAY?

☆ ☆ ☆ ☆ ☆

# Thursday

DATE:

TODAY I FELT

## WHAT WAS ON MY MIND TODAY? HOW DID IT MAKE ME FEEL?

___________________________________________

___________________________________________

___________________________________________

___________________________________________

___________________________________________

## WHAT WENT WELL TODAY?

_______________________________

_______________________________

_______________________________

_______________________________

_______________________________

_______________________________

_______________________________

_______________________________

## TODAY DID I...

○ SMILE

○ MEDITATE

○ EXERCISE

○ EAT NUTRITIOUS FOOD

○ CATCH FRESH AIR

○ SPEND TIME WITH THE
  PEOPLE I LOVE

○ SLEEP WELL

## THREE THINGS I AM GRATEFUL FOR

_______________________________

_______________________________

_______________________________

_______________________________

_______________________________

## I APPRECIATE MYSELF FOR

DID ANYTHING TRIGGER MY ANXIETY TODAY?

HOW DID I DEAL WITH IT?

HOW CAN I REFRAME MY ANXIOUS THOUGHTS TO FEEL BETTER?

THE BEST THING ABOUT TODAY

WHAT AM I EXCITED ABOUT FOR TOMORROW?

HOW WELL DID I MANAGE MY ANXIETY TODAY?

☆ ☆ ☆ ☆ ☆

# Friday

DATE:

TODAY I FELT

WHAT WAS ON MY MIND TODAY? HOW DID IT MAKE ME FEEL?

_______________________________________________

_______________________________________________

_______________________________________________

_______________________________________________

_______________________________________________

## WHAT WENT WELL TODAY?

_________________________________

_________________________________

_________________________________

_________________________________

_________________________________

_________________________________

_________________________________

_________________________________

_________________________________

## TODAY DID I...

○ SMILE

○ MEDITATE

○ EXERCISE

○ EAT NUTRITIOUS FOOD

○ CATCH FRESH AIR

○ SPEND TIME WITH THE PEOPLE I LOVE

○ SLEEP WELL

## THREE THINGS I AM GRATEFUL FOR

_________________________________

_________________________________

_________________________________

_________________________________

_________________________________

_________________________________

## I APPRECIATE MYSELF FOR

DID ANYTHING TRIGGER MY ANXIETY TODAY?

HOW DID I DEAL WITH IT?

HOW CAN I REFRAME MY ANXIOUS THOUGHTS TO FEEL BETTER?

THE BEST THING ABOUT TODAY

WHAT AM I EXCITED ABOUT FOR TOMORROW?

HOW WELL DID I MANAGE MY ANXIETY TODAY?

☆ ☆ ☆ ☆ ☆

# Saturday

DATE:

TODAY I FELT

WHAT WAS ON MY MIND TODAY? HOW DID IT MAKE ME FEEL?

_______________________________________________

_______________________________________________

_______________________________________________

_______________________________________________

_______________________________________________

## WHAT WENT WELL TODAY?

_________________________________

_________________________________

_________________________________

_________________________________

_________________________________

_________________________________

_________________________________

_________________________________

_________________________________

## TODAY DID I...

- ○ SMILE
- ○ MEDITATE
- ○ EXERCISE
- ○ EAT NUTRITIOUS FOOD
- ○ CATCH FRESH AIR
- ○ SPEND TIME WITH THE PEOPLE I LOVE
- ○ SLEEP WELL

## THREE THINGS I AM GRATEFUL FOR

_________________________________

_________________________________

_________________________________

_________________________________

_________________________________

_________________________________

## I APPRECIATE MYSELF FOR

DID ANYTHING TRIGGER MY ANXIETY TODAY?

_______________________________________

_______________________________________

_______________________________________

_______________________________________

_______________________________________

HOW DID I DEAL WITH IT?

_______________________________________

_______________________________________

_______________________________________

_______________________________________

_______________________________________

HOW CAN I REFRAME MY ANXIOUS THOUGHTS TO FEEL BETTER?

_______________________________________

_______________________________________

_______________________________________

_______________________________________

_______________________________________

THE BEST THING ABOUT TODAY

______________________________

______________________________

______________________________

______________________________

______________________________

______________________________

WHAT AM I EXCITED ABOUT FOR TOMORROW?

HOW WELL DID I MANAGE MY ANXIETY TODAY?

☆ ☆ ☆ ☆ ☆

# Sunday

DATE:

TODAY I FELT
___________________________

## WHAT WAS ON MY MIND TODAY? HOW DID IT MAKE ME FEEL?

_______________________________________________

_______________________________________________

_______________________________________________

_______________________________________________

## WHAT WENT WELL TODAY?

_________________________________

_________________________________

_________________________________

_________________________________

_________________________________

_________________________________

_________________________________

_________________________________

## TODAY DID I...

○ SMILE

○ MEDITATE

○ EXERCISE

○ EAT NUTRITIOUS FOOD

○ CATCH FRESH AIR

○ SPEND TIME WITH THE PEOPLE I LOVE

○ SLEEP WELL

## THREE THINGS I AM GRATEFUL FOR

_________________________________

_________________________________

_________________________________

_________________________________

_________________________________

_________________________________

## I APPRECIATE MYSELF FOR

DID ANYTHING TRIGGER MY ANXIETY TODAY?

_______________________________________________

_______________________________________________

_______________________________________________

_______________________________________________

HOW DID I DEAL WITH IT?

_______________________________________________

_______________________________________________

_______________________________________________

_______________________________________________

HOW CAN I REFRAME MY ANXIOUS THOUGHTS TO FEEL BETTER?

_______________________________________________

_______________________________________________

_______________________________________________

_______________________________________________

THE BEST THING ABOUT TODAY

_______________________________

_______________________________

_______________________________

_______________________________

_______________________________

_______________________________

WHAT AM I EXCITED ABOUT FOR TOMORROW?

HOW WELL DID I MANAGE MY ANXIETY TODAY?

☆ ☆ ☆ ☆ ☆

DATE:

WHAT DID I DO WELL THIS WEEK?

_______________________________________________

_______________________________________________

_______________________________________________

_______________________________________________

THIS WEEK I FELT

HOW WELL DID I MANAGE MY
ANXIETY THIS WEEK?

☆ ☆ ☆ ☆ ☆

WHAT DID I DO WELL THIS WEEK?

_______________________________________________

_______________________________________________

_______________________________________________

_______________________________________________

WHAT WOULD I LIKE TO DO
BETTER NEXT WEEK?

WHAT AM I EXCITED ABOUT IN
THE UPCOMING WEEK?

# Month 2
# Check in

## HOW WELL DID I MANAGE MY ANXIETY THIS MONTH?

## HOW DO I FEEL ABOUT THIS MONTH?

_______________________________________________

_______________________________________________

_______________________________________________

## MY ACCOMPLISHMENTS THIS MONTH

1

2

3

## WHAT HELPED ME STAY CALM THIS MONTH?

_______________________________________________

_______________________________________________

_______________________________________________

_______________________________________________

## HOW HAVE I GROWN THIS MONTH?

_______________________________

_______________________________

_______________________________

_______________________________

_______________________________

## WHAT DO I WANT TO DO DIFFERENTLY NEXT MONTH?

_______________________________

_______________________________

_______________________________

_______________________________

_______________________________

# Let's Color

# Circle of Influence

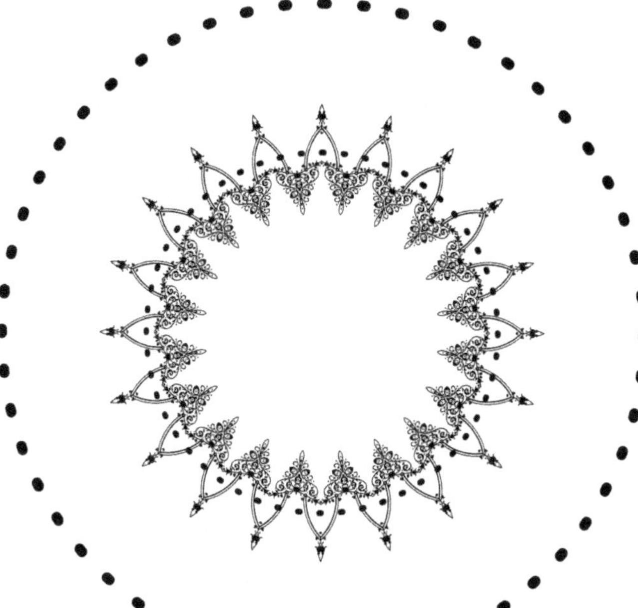

"
IF YOU ARE NOT EXCITED
ABOUT IT, IT'S NOT THE
RIGHT PATH
– ABRAHAM HICKS

# Circle of Influence

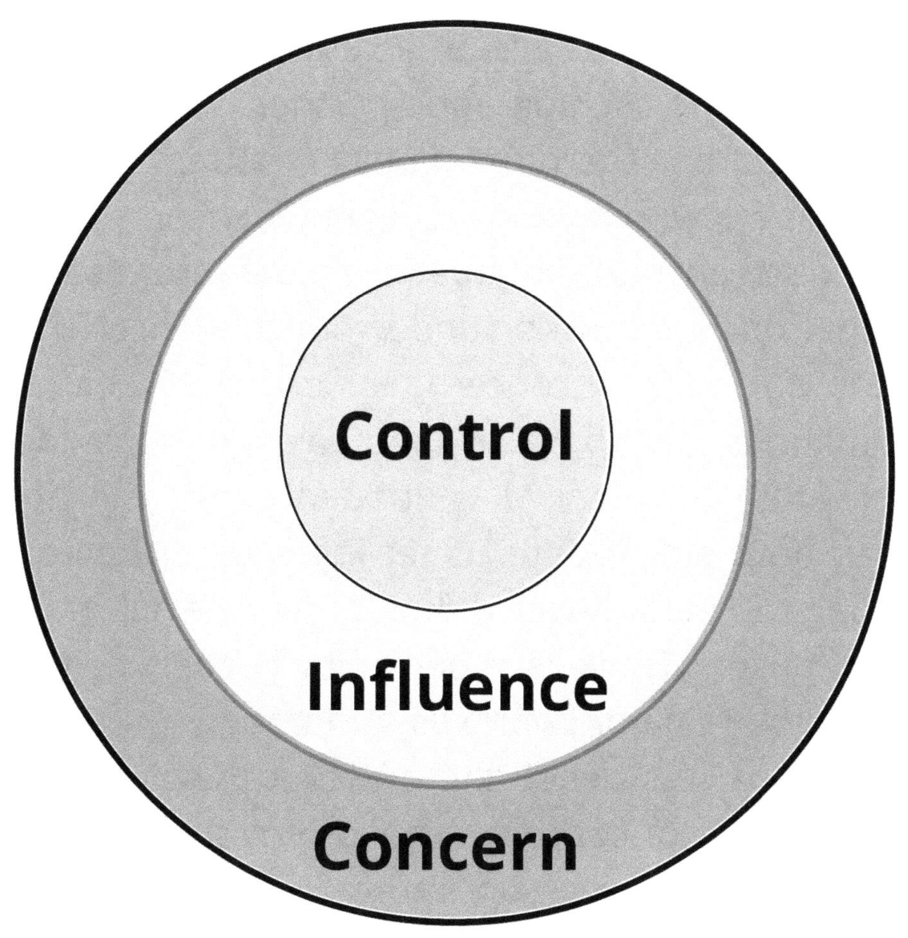



Your circle of control encompasses everything that is within your control, such as your thoughts, feelings, and behaviors. For instance, you have the ability to make decisions about staying in a job, starting a business, or being in a relationship. Hence, these lie in your circle of control.

There are also people, situations, and circumstances that you cannot directly control but can influence. For example, you can influence your colleagues to accept a decision, or you can work toward aligning your partner's perspective with yours regarding family matters. These aspects fall within your circle of influence.

We also encounter situations that are neither within our control nor under our influence. They lie in our circle of concern. For example, weather conditions, health issues, and calamities may not be within our control or influence. Focusing on their downsides keeps us feeling stuck. When our hiking trip gets canceled due to rain, it's natural to feel upset. However, becoming upset neither stops the rain nor improves our mood.

Therefore, it is beneficial to accept things that lie in our circle of concern instead of resisting them. By doing so, we gain more control over our emotions and become better equipped to find alternative solutions.

Let's say you are feeling anxious because of someone's curt behavior towards you. In this situation, what is within your control is your own thoughts and behavior, not theirs. By focusing on what's inside your circle of control, you can reclaim your power and expand your circle of influence.

When you remain calm and composed, you are better able to make thoughtful decisions and respond to situations instead of reacting impulsively. This self-awareness can have an impact on the people who may not be treating you well. It might nudge them to re-evaluate their behavior towards you.

By prioritizing your emotional well-being and focusing on what you can control, you can create a positive shift in your interactions and influence others to treat you better. This kind of introspection on their part would not have been possible if you had focused on trying to control their behavior instead of working on your response.

*When you control what's in your control, what's not in your control also starts to come under your control, thereby, expanding your circle of influence.*

# Discovering your circle of influence

Take a situation that makes you anxious and ask yourself:

What elements of this situation are in my control?

___________________________

___________________________

___________________________

What are the three things that lie inside my circle of influence that I can work on?

___________________________

___________________________

___________________________

How will working more on these areas help me?

___________________________

___________________________

___________________________

___________________________

What specific actions can I take on these areas right away?

________________________________

________________________________

________________________________

What is outside my circle of control?

________________________________

________________________________

________________________________

Am I focused on things outside my control?

________________________________

________________________________

________________________________

If I can't control things what happens to me?

________________________________

________________________________

________________________________

# Monday

DATE:

TODAY I FELT

WHAT WAS ON MY MIND TODAY? HOW DID IT MAKE ME FEEL?

WHAT WENT WELL TODAY?

TODAY DID I...

- SMILE
- MEDITATE
- EXERCISE
- EAT NUTRITIOUS FOOD
- CATCH FRESH AIR
- SPEND TIME WITH THE PEOPLE I LOVE
- SLEEP WELL

THREE THINGS I AM GRATEFUL FOR

I APPRECIATE MYSELF FOR

DID ANYTHING TRIGGER MY ANXIETY TODAY?

_______________________________________________

_______________________________________________

_______________________________________________

_______________________________________________

HOW DID I DEAL WITH IT?

_______________________________________________

_______________________________________________

_______________________________________________

_______________________________________________

HOW CAN I REFRAME MY ANXIOUS THOUGHTS TO FEEL BETTER?

_______________________________________________

_______________________________________________

_______________________________________________

_______________________________________________

THE BEST THING ABOUT TODAY

_______________________________

_______________________________

_______________________________

_______________________________

_______________________________

_______________________________

_______________________________

WHAT AM I EXCITED ABOUT FOR TOMORROW?

HOW WELL DID I MANAGE MY ANXIETY TODAY?

☆ ☆ ☆ ☆ ☆

# Tuesday

DATE:

TODAY I FELT

WHAT WAS ON MY MIND TODAY? HOW DID IT MAKE ME FEEL?

__________________________________________________

__________________________________________________

__________________________________________________

__________________________________________________

__________________________________________________

WHAT WENT WELL TODAY?

__________________________________

__________________________________

__________________________________

__________________________________

__________________________________

__________________________________

__________________________________

__________________________________

__________________________________

TODAY DID I...

- ○ SMILE
- ○ MEDITATE
- ○ EXERCISE
- ○ EAT NUTRITIOUS FOOD
- ○ CATCH FRESH AIR
- ○ SPEND TIME WITH THE PEOPLE I LOVE
- ○ SLEEP WELL

THREE THINGS I AM GRATEFUL FOR

__________________________________

__________________________________

__________________________________

__________________________________

__________________________________

__________________________________

I APPRECIATE MYSELF FOR

DID ANYTHING TRIGGER MY ANXIETY TODAY?

_______________________________________________

_______________________________________________

_______________________________________________

_______________________________________________

HOW DID I DEAL WITH IT?

_______________________________________________

_______________________________________________

_______________________________________________

_______________________________________________

HOW CAN I REFRAME MY ANXIOUS THOUGHTS TO FEEL BETTER?

_______________________________________________

_______________________________________________

_______________________________________________

_______________________________________________

THE BEST THING ABOUT TODAY

_______________________________

_______________________________

_______________________________

_______________________________

_______________________________

_______________________________

WHAT AM I EXCITED ABOUT FOR TOMORROW?

HOW WELL DID I MANAGE MY ANXIETY TODAY?

☆ ☆ ☆ ☆ ☆

# Wednesday

DATE:

TODAY I FELT
_______________________

WHAT WAS ON MY MIND TODAY? HOW DID IT MAKE ME FEEL?

_______________________________________________

_______________________________________________

_______________________________________________

_______________________________________________

_______________________________________________

WHAT WENT WELL TODAY?

___________________________________

___________________________________

___________________________________

___________________________________

___________________________________

___________________________________

___________________________________

___________________________________

___________________________________

TODAY DID I...

○ SMILE

○ MEDITATE

○ EXERCISE

○ EAT NUTRITIOUS FOOD

○ CATCH FRESH AIR

○ SPEND TIME WITH THE
  PEOPLE I LOVE

○ SLEEP WELL

THREE THINGS I AM GRATEFUL FOR

___________________________________

___________________________________

___________________________________

___________________________________

___________________________________

___________________________________

I APPRECIATE MYSELF FOR

DID ANYTHING TRIGGER MY ANXIETY TODAY?

_______________________________________________

_______________________________________________

_______________________________________________

_______________________________________________

_______________________________________________

HOW DID I DEAL WITH IT?

_______________________________________________

_______________________________________________

_______________________________________________

_______________________________________________

_______________________________________________

HOW CAN I REFRAME MY ANXIOUS THOUGHTS TO FEEL BETTER?

_______________________________________________

_______________________________________________

_______________________________________________

_______________________________________________

_______________________________________________

THE BEST THING ABOUT TODAY

______________________________

______________________________

______________________________

______________________________

______________________________

______________________________

WHAT AM I EXCITED ABOUT FOR TOMORROW?

HOW WELL DID I MANAGE MY ANXIETY TODAY?

☆ ☆ ☆ ☆ ☆

# Thursday

DATE:

TODAY I FELT
______________________________________

## WHAT WAS ON MY MIND TODAY? HOW DID IT MAKE ME FEEL?

______________________________________
______________________________________
______________________________________
______________________________________

## WHAT WENT WELL TODAY?

______________________________________
______________________________________
______________________________________
______________________________________
______________________________________
______________________________________
______________________________________
______________________________________

## TODAY DID I...

○ SMILE

○ MEDITATE

○ EXERCISE

○ EAT NUTRITIOUS FOOD

○ CATCH FRESH AIR

○ SPEND TIME WITH THE PEOPLE I LOVE

○ SLEEP WELL

## THREE THINGS I AM GRATEFUL FOR

______________________________________
______________________________________
______________________________________
______________________________________
______________________________________

## I APPRECIATE MYSELF FOR

DID ANYTHING TRIGGER MY ANXIETY TODAY?

_______________________________________

_______________________________________

_______________________________________

_______________________________________

HOW DID I DEAL WITH IT?

_______________________________________

_______________________________________

_______________________________________

_______________________________________

HOW CAN I REFRAME MY ANXIOUS THOUGHTS TO FEEL BETTER?

_______________________________________

_______________________________________

_______________________________________

_______________________________________

THE BEST THING ABOUT TODAY

_______________________________

_______________________________

_______________________________

_______________________________

_______________________________

_______________________________

WHAT AM I EXCITED ABOUT FOR TOMORROW?

HOW WELL DID I MANAGE MY ANXIETY TODAY?

☆ ☆ ☆ ☆ ☆

# Friday

DATE:

TODAY I FELT
___________________________

## WHAT WAS ON MY MIND TODAY? HOW DID IT MAKE ME FEEL?

_______________________________________________

_______________________________________________

_______________________________________________

_______________________________________________

_______________________________________________

## WHAT WENT WELL TODAY?

__________________________________

__________________________________

__________________________________

__________________________________

__________________________________

__________________________________

__________________________________

__________________________________

__________________________________

## TODAY DID I...

○ SMILE

○ MEDITATE

○ EXERCISE

○ EAT NUTRITIOUS FOOD

○ CATCH FRESH AIR

○ SPEND TIME WITH THE PEOPLE I LOVE

○ SLEEP WELL

## THREE THINGS I AM GRATEFUL FOR

__________________________________

__________________________________

__________________________________

__________________________________

__________________________________

__________________________________

## I APPRECIATE MYSELF FOR

DID ANYTHING TRIGGER MY ANXIETY TODAY?

___________________________________________

___________________________________________

___________________________________________

___________________________________________

___________________________________________

HOW DID I DEAL WITH IT?

___________________________________________

___________________________________________

___________________________________________

___________________________________________

___________________________________________

HOW CAN I REFRAME MY ANXIOUS THOUGHTS TO FEEL BETTER?

___________________________________________

___________________________________________

___________________________________________

___________________________________________

___________________________________________

THE BEST THING ABOUT TODAY

_________________________________

_________________________________

_________________________________

_________________________________

_________________________________

_________________________________

WHAT AM I EXCITED ABOUT FOR TOMORROW?

HOW WELL DID I MANAGE MY ANXIETY TODAY?

☆ ☆ ☆ ☆ ☆

# Saturday

DATE:

TODAY I FELT

## WHAT WAS ON MY MIND TODAY? HOW DID IT MAKE ME FEEL?

______________________________________________

______________________________________________

______________________________________________

______________________________________________

## WHAT WENT WELL TODAY?

________________________________

________________________________

________________________________

________________________________

________________________________

________________________________

________________________________

________________________________

## TODAY DID I...

○ SMILE

○ MEDITATE

○ EXERCISE

○ EAT NUTRITIOUS FOOD

○ CATCH FRESH AIR

○ SPEND TIME WITH THE PEOPLE I LOVE

○ SLEEP WELL

## THREE THINGS I AM GRATEFUL FOR

________________________________

________________________________

________________________________

________________________________

________________________________

## I APPRECIATE MYSELF FOR

DID ANYTHING TRIGGER MY ANXIETY TODAY?

HOW DID I DEAL WITH IT?

HOW CAN I REFRAME MY ANXIOUS THOUGHTS TO FEEL BETTER?

THE BEST THING ABOUT TODAY

WHAT AM I EXCITED ABOUT FOR TOMORROW?

HOW WELL DID I MANAGE MY ANXIETY TODAY?

☆ ☆ ☆ ☆ ☆

# Sunday

DATE:

TODAY I FELT

WHAT WAS ON MY MIND TODAY? HOW DID IT MAKE ME FEEL?

______________________________________________

______________________________________________

______________________________________________

______________________________________________

## WHAT WENT WELL TODAY?

________________________________

________________________________

________________________________

________________________________

________________________________

________________________________

________________________________

________________________________

________________________________

## TODAY DID I...

- ○ SMILE
- ○ MEDITATE
- ○ EXERCISE
- ○ EAT NUTRITIOUS FOOD
- ○ CATCH FRESH AIR
- ○ SPEND TIME WITH THE PEOPLE I LOVE
- ○ SLEEP WELL

## THREE THINGS I AM GRATEFUL FOR

________________________________

________________________________

________________________________

________________________________

________________________________

________________________________

## I APPRECIATE MYSELF FOR

DID ANYTHING TRIGGER MY ANXIETY TODAY?

_______________________________________

_______________________________________

_______________________________________

_______________________________________

HOW DID I DEAL WITH IT?

_______________________________________

_______________________________________

_______________________________________

_______________________________________

HOW CAN I REFRAME MY ANXIOUS THOUGHTS TO FEEL BETTER?

_______________________________________

_______________________________________

_______________________________________

_______________________________________

THE BEST THING ABOUT TODAY

___________________________

___________________________

___________________________

___________________________

___________________________

___________________________

WHAT AM I EXCITED ABOUT FOR TOMORROW?

HOW WELL DID I MANAGE MY ANXIETY TODAY?

☆ ☆ ☆ ☆ ☆

# Week 9
# Check in

WHAT DID I DO WELL THIS WEEK?

_______________________________________________

_______________________________________________

_______________________________________________

_______________________________________________

THIS WEEK I FELT

HOW WELL DID I MANAGE MY ANXIETY THIS WEEK?

☆ ☆ ☆ ☆ ☆

WHAT DID I DO WELL THIS WEEK?

_______________________________________________

_______________________________________________

_______________________________________________

_______________________________________________

WHAT WOULD I LIKE TO DO BETTER NEXT WEEK?

WHAT AM I EXCITED ABOUT IN THE UPCOMING WEEK?

# Time Structuring

THE MORE WE LOVE
OURSELVES THE LESS WE
PROJECT OUR PAIN ONTO
THE WORLD
– LOUISE HAY

# Time Structuring

One effective method to overcome anxiety is by being mindful of how we spend our time. Engaging in productive activities allows us to channel our energy toward tasks that contribute to the attainment of our objectives.

As we make strides toward achieving our goals, we cultivate a sense of competence and self-assurance, which, in turn, reduces anxiety. Furthermore, by keeping ourselves occupied with purposeful endeavors, we have less time available for overthinking, which is a common trigger for anxiety.

It is also important to incorporate relaxation activities into our routine. These can include spending quality time with loved ones, practicing self-care, or pursuing leisurely interests. These activities provide a much-needed break from the daily demands of life and help us rejuvenate.

By consciously structuring our time and maintaining a healthy equilibrium between productive and relaxing activities, we can effectively manage anxiety.

# It's pie time!

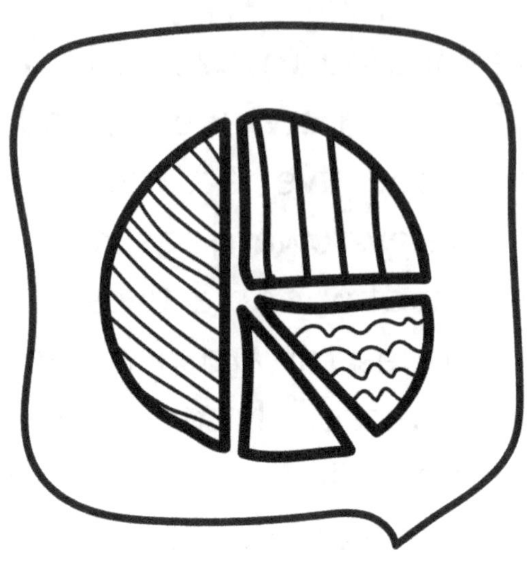

Use the circle on the following page to demarcate your daily activities. If you spend more time on a particular activity, make the corresponding slice in the pie larger. That way, each slice will be proportionate to the time dedicated to that activity, visually representing a comparison between the different activities.

In each section, write down the category name followed by the specific activities you spend time on in that category. For example, under "Rest and relaxation activities," you can note down activities such as taking an afternoon power nap or practicing morning meditation. Additionally, you can refer to the section on "Mindfulness" and include any mindfulness activities you are practicing.

# Your time structuring pie chart

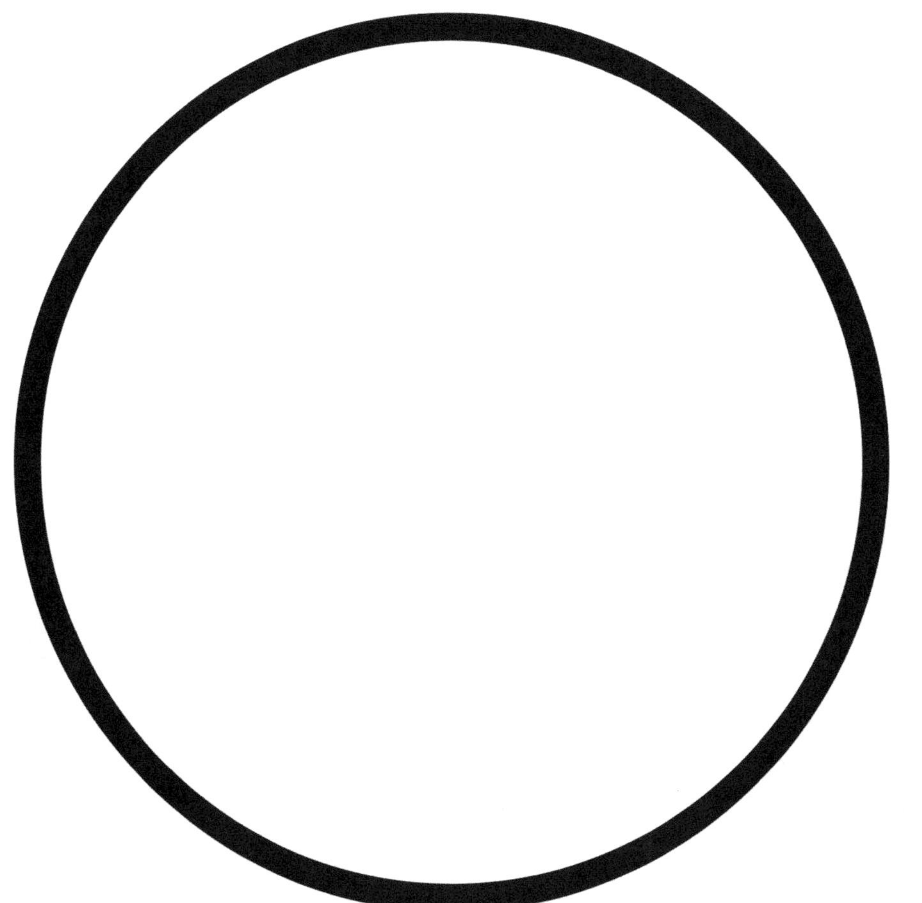

Educational activities
Social media activities
Rest and relaxation activities
Eating activities
Personal grooming
Leisure and sports
Job activities
Any other? Please mention.

**(*Please a different color for each category*)**

# Your new time structuring pie chart

Do you want to structure your time better? Draw another pie chart depicting how you would like your time structure pie to be.

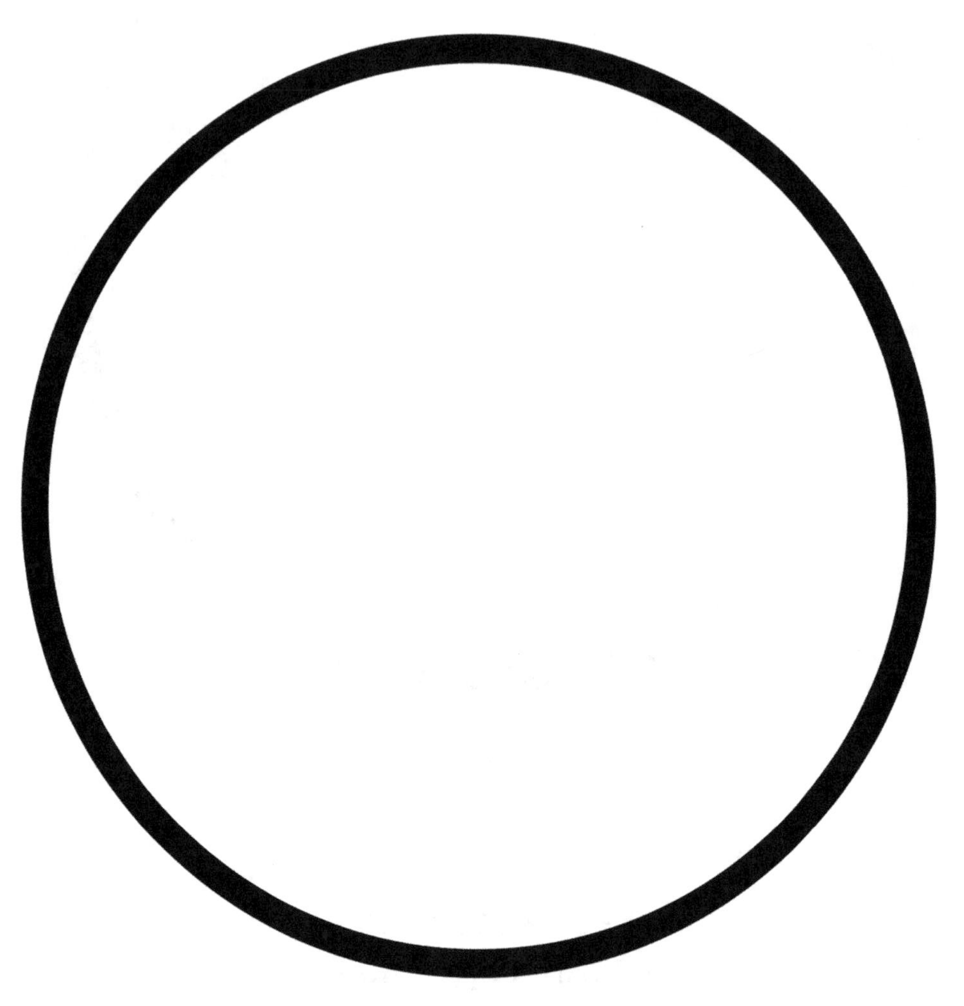

Which activities have you introduced in your new pie chart?

_______________________________________________

_______________________________________________

_______________________________________________

Which activities have you removed from the old pie chart?

_______________________________________________

_______________________________________________

_______________________________________________

Mention three daily actions you can take to change your pie chart from the way it is to the way you want it to be.

_______________________________________________

_______________________________________________

_______________________________________________

*Visualize the changes in your life once your time is structured differently!*

# Monday

DATE:

TODAY I FELT

## WHAT WAS ON MY MIND TODAY? HOW DID IT MAKE ME FEEL?

______________________________________________

______________________________________________

______________________________________________

______________________________________________

______________________________________________

## WHAT WENT WELL TODAY?

______________________________

______________________________

______________________________

______________________________

______________________________

______________________________

______________________________

______________________________

______________________________

## TODAY DID I...

○ SMILE

○ MEDITATE

○ EXERCISE

○ EAT NUTRITIOUS FOOD

○ CATCH FRESH AIR

○ SPEND TIME WITH THE
PEOPLE I LOVE

○ SLEEP WELL

## THREE THINGS I AM GRATEFUL FOR

______________________________

______________________________

______________________________

______________________________

______________________________

## I APPRECIATE MYSELF FOR

DID ANYTHING TRIGGER MY ANXIETY TODAY?

HOW DID I DEAL WITH IT?

HOW CAN I REFRAME MY ANXIOUS THOUGHTS TO FEEL BETTER?

THE BEST THING ABOUT TODAY

WHAT AM I EXCITED ABOUT FOR TOMORROW?

HOW WELL DID I MANAGE MY ANXIETY TODAY?

☆ ☆ ☆ ☆ ☆

# Tuesday

DATE:

TODAY I FELT

WHAT WAS ON MY MIND TODAY? HOW DID IT MAKE ME FEEL?

_______________________________________________

_______________________________________________

_______________________________________________

_______________________________________________

## WHAT WENT WELL TODAY?

_______________________________

_______________________________

_______________________________

_______________________________

_______________________________

_______________________________

_______________________________

## TODAY DID I...

○ SMILE

○ MEDITATE

○ EXERCISE

○ EAT NUTRITIOUS FOOD

○ CATCH FRESH AIR

○ SPEND TIME WITH THE
PEOPLE I LOVE

○ SLEEP WELL

## THREE THINGS I AM GRATEFUL FOR

_______________________________

_______________________________

_______________________________

_______________________________

_______________________________

## I APPRECIATE MYSELF FOR

DID ANYTHING TRIGGER MY ANXIETY TODAY?

_______________________________________________

_______________________________________________

_______________________________________________

_______________________________________________

_______________________________________________

HOW DID I DEAL WITH IT?

_______________________________________________

_______________________________________________

_______________________________________________

_______________________________________________

_______________________________________________

HOW CAN I REFRAME MY ANXIOUS THOUGHTS TO FEEL BETTER?

_______________________________________________

_______________________________________________

_______________________________________________

_______________________________________________

_______________________________________________

THE BEST THING ABOUT TODAY

_______________________________

_______________________________

_______________________________

_______________________________

_______________________________

_______________________________

WHAT AM I EXCITED ABOUT FOR TOMORROW?

HOW WELL DID I MANAGE MY ANXIETY TODAY?

☆ ☆ ☆ ☆ ☆

# Wednesday

DATE:

TODAY I FELT

## WHAT WAS ON MY MIND TODAY? HOW DID IT MAKE ME FEEL?

_______________________________________________

_______________________________________________

_______________________________________________

_______________________________________________

## WHAT WENT WELL TODAY?

_________________________________

_________________________________

_________________________________

_________________________________

_________________________________

_________________________________

_________________________________

## TODAY DID I...

○ SMILE

○ MEDITATE

○ EXERCISE

○ EAT NUTRITIOUS FOOD

○ CATCH FRESH AIR

○ SPEND TIME WITH THE PEOPLE I LOVE

○ SLEEP WELL

## THREE THINGS I AM GRATEFUL FOR

_________________________________

_________________________________

_________________________________

_________________________________

_________________________________

_________________________________

## I APPRECIATE MYSELF FOR

## DID ANYTHING TRIGGER MY ANXIETY TODAY?

## HOW DID I DEAL WITH IT?

## HOW CAN I REFRAME MY ANXIOUS THOUGHTS TO FEEL BETTER?

## THE BEST THING ABOUT TODAY

## WHAT AM I EXCITED ABOUT FOR TOMORROW?

## HOW WELL DID I MANAGE MY ANXIETY TODAY?

☆ ☆ ☆ ☆ ☆

# Thursday

DATE:

TODAY I FELT

WHAT WAS ON MY MIND TODAY? HOW DID IT MAKE ME FEEL?

______________________________________________

______________________________________________

______________________________________________

______________________________________________

______________________________________________

## WHAT WENT WELL TODAY?

______________________________

______________________________

______________________________

______________________________

______________________________

______________________________

______________________________

______________________________

## TODAY DID I...

○ SMILE

○ MEDITATE

○ EXERCISE

○ EAT NUTRITIOUS FOOD

○ CATCH FRESH AIR

○ SPEND TIME WITH THE PEOPLE I LOVE

○ SLEEP WELL

## THREE THINGS I AM GRATEFUL FOR

______________________________

______________________________

______________________________

______________________________

______________________________

## I APPRECIATE MYSELF FOR

DID ANYTHING TRIGGER MY ANXIETY TODAY?

_______________________________________________

_______________________________________________

_______________________________________________

_______________________________________________

_______________________________________________

HOW DID I DEAL WITH IT?

_______________________________________________

_______________________________________________

_______________________________________________

_______________________________________________

_______________________________________________

HOW CAN I REFRAME MY ANXIOUS THOUGHTS TO FEEL BETTER?

_______________________________________________

_______________________________________________

_______________________________________________

_______________________________________________

_______________________________________________

THE BEST THING ABOUT TODAY

_______________________________

_______________________________

_______________________________

_______________________________

_______________________________

_______________________________

WHAT AM I EXCITED ABOUT FOR TOMORROW?

HOW WELL DID I MANAGE MY ANXIETY TODAY?

☆ ☆ ☆ ☆ ☆

# Friday

DATE:

TODAY I FELT

## WHAT WAS ON MY MIND TODAY? HOW DID IT MAKE ME FEEL?

______________________________________________

______________________________________________

______________________________________________

______________________________________________

______________________________________________

## WHAT WENT WELL TODAY?

## TODAY DID I...

○ SMILE

○ MEDITATE

○ EXERCISE

○ EAT NUTRITIOUS FOOD

○ CATCH FRESH AIR

○ SPEND TIME WITH THE PEOPLE I LOVE

○ SLEEP WELL

## THREE THINGS I AM GRATEFUL FOR

## I APPRECIATE MYSELF FOR

DID ANYTHING TRIGGER MY ANXIETY TODAY?

HOW DID I DEAL WITH IT?

HOW CAN I REFRAME MY ANXIOUS THOUGHTS TO FEEL BETTER?

THE BEST THING ABOUT TODAY

WHAT AM I EXCITED ABOUT FOR TOMORROW?

HOW WELL DID I MANAGE MY ANXIETY TODAY?

☆ ☆ ☆ ☆ ☆

# Saturday

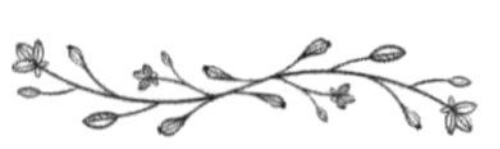

DATE:

TODAY I FELT

WHAT WAS ON MY MIND TODAY? HOW DID IT MAKE ME FEEL?

___________________________________________

___________________________________________

___________________________________________

___________________________________________

WHAT WENT WELL TODAY?

_______________________________

_______________________________

_______________________________

_______________________________

_______________________________

_______________________________

_______________________________

_______________________________

TODAY DID I...

○ SMILE

○ MEDITATE

○ EXERCISE

○ EAT NUTRITIOUS FOOD

○ CATCH FRESH AIR

○ SPEND TIME WITH THE
PEOPLE I LOVE

○ SLEEP WELL

THREE THINGS I AM GRATEFUL FOR

_______________________________

_______________________________

_______________________________

_______________________________

_______________________________

_______________________________

I APPRECIATE MYSELF FOR

DID ANYTHING TRIGGER MY ANXIETY TODAY?

_______________________________________________

_______________________________________________

_______________________________________________

_______________________________________________

_______________________________________________

HOW DID I DEAL WITH IT?

_______________________________________________

_______________________________________________

_______________________________________________

_______________________________________________

_______________________________________________

HOW CAN I REFRAME MY ANXIOUS THOUGHTS TO FEEL BETTER?

_______________________________________________

_______________________________________________

_______________________________________________

_______________________________________________

_______________________________________________

THE BEST THING ABOUT TODAY

_______________________________

_______________________________

_______________________________

_______________________________

_______________________________

_______________________________

WHAT AM I EXCITED ABOUT FOR TOMORROW?

HOW WELL DID I MANAGE MY ANXIETY TODAY?

☆ ☆ ☆ ☆ ☆

# Sunday

DATE:

TODAY I FELT
_______________________________

## WHAT WAS ON MY MIND TODAY? HOW DID IT MAKE ME FEEL?

_______________________________________________________

_______________________________________________________

_______________________________________________________

_______________________________________________________

## WHAT WENT WELL TODAY?

___________________________________

___________________________________

___________________________________

___________________________________

___________________________________

___________________________________

___________________________________

___________________________________

## TODAY DID I...

○ SMILE

○ MEDITATE

○ EXERCISE

○ EAT NUTRITIOUS FOOD

○ CATCH FRESH AIR

○ SPEND TIME WITH THE
  PEOPLE I LOVE

○ SLEEP WELL

## THREE THINGS I AM GRATEFUL FOR

___________________________________

___________________________________

___________________________________

___________________________________

___________________________________

## I APPRECIATE MYSELF FOR

DID ANYTHING TRIGGER MY ANXIETY TODAY?

HOW DID I DEAL WITH IT?

HOW CAN I REFRAME MY ANXIOUS THOUGHTS TO FEEL BETTER?

THE BEST THING ABOUT TODAY

WHAT AM I EXCITED ABOUT FOR TOMORROW?

HOW WELL DID I MANAGE MY ANXIETY TODAY?

☆ ☆ ☆ ☆ ☆

# Week 10
# Check in

WHAT DID I DO WELL THIS WEEK?

______________________________

______________________________

______________________________

______________________________

THIS WEEK I FELT

HOW WELL DID I MANAGE MY ANXIETY THIS WEEK?

☆ ☆ ☆ ☆ ☆

WHAT DID I DO WELL THIS WEEK?

______________________________

______________________________

______________________________

______________________________

WHAT WOULD I LIKE TO DO BETTER NEXT WEEK?

WHAT AM I EXCITED ABOUT IN THE UPCOMING WEEK?

# Where do you Feel it in Your Body?

66

IT DOESN'T MATTER HOW
SLOWLY YOU GO AS LONG
AS YOU DO NOT STOP
– CONFUCIUS

# Where do you Feel it in Your Body?

Pain and pleasure, fundamentally, are mental representations of our experiences. The anxiety we encounter is stored in our bodies as energy. To alleviate this anxiety, we need to focus on releasing the energy linked to it.

Let's explore a bodywork practice that can assist us in achieving this goal.

## Guidelines

- Perform this exercise when you are alone.
- Take a few deep breaths before beginning.
- The results depend on your level of focus and absorption in the process.
- Memorize the sequence of steps beforehand so that you can perform the exercise with your eyes closed.
- If you find it difficult to memorize the steps, consider recording the instructions as an audio file. You can then play back the guided tape to do the exercise.

(This exercise is based on the work of hypnotherapist David Snyder)

# Exercise to remove the energy of anxiety

- Where do you feel the anxiety in your body? Your gut, chest, head, or somewhere else?
- What color is it?
- Pull out the color with both hands and place it in front of your body. Continue this until you get all the color out.
- Which direction is the energy spinning?
- What color would you like to change it to if you were to convert it to peace?
- Which direction would peace spin?
- Imagine it spinning at full speed in the chosen direction with the associated color.
- Once it gains sufficient momentum slam the energy back into your body.
- Notice that you are healed. Notice that it's gone. Try to bring it back and notice what happens instead.

How were you feeling before the exercise?

How are you feeling after the exercise?

Did something change?

If so, where do you feel the change in your body? describe the change.

# Color Your Energy

Color the place where you experience anxiety in your body. Use the color you associate with anxiety.

Change the color to one that represents calm to you.

# Let's Color

# Monday

DATE:

TODAY I FELT
_______________________

## WHAT WAS ON MY MIND TODAY? HOW DID IT MAKE ME FEEL?

_________________________________________________

_________________________________________________

_________________________________________________

_________________________________________________

## WHAT WENT WELL TODAY?

_______________________________

_______________________________

_______________________________

_______________________________

_______________________________

_______________________________

_______________________________

## TODAY DID I...

- ○ SMILE
- ○ MEDITATE
- ○ EXERCISE
- ○ EAT NUTRITIOUS FOOD
- ○ CATCH FRESH AIR
- ○ SPEND TIME WITH THE PEOPLE I LOVE
- ○ SLEEP WELL

## THREE THINGS I AM GRATEFUL FOR

_______________________________

_______________________________

_______________________________

_______________________________

_______________________________

_______________________________

## I APPRECIATE MYSELF FOR

DID ANYTHING TRIGGER MY ANXIETY TODAY?

HOW DID I DEAL WITH IT?

HOW CAN I REFRAME MY ANXIOUS THOUGHTS TO FEEL BETTER?

THE BEST THING ABOUT TODAY

WHAT AM I EXCITED ABOUT FOR TOMORROW?

HOW WELL DID I MANAGE MY ANXIETY TODAY?

# Tuesday

DATE:

TODAY I FELT

## WHAT WAS ON MY MIND TODAY? HOW DID IT MAKE ME FEEL?

________________________________________

________________________________________

________________________________________

________________________________________

________________________________________

## WHAT WENT WELL TODAY?

________________________________

________________________________

________________________________

________________________________

________________________________

________________________________

________________________________

________________________________

________________________________

## TODAY DID I...

○ SMILE

○ MEDITATE

○ EXERCISE

○ EAT NUTRITIOUS FOOD

○ CATCH FRESH AIR

○ SPEND TIME WITH THE PEOPLE I LOVE

○ SLEEP WELL

## THREE THINGS I AM GRATEFUL FOR

________________________________

________________________________

________________________________

________________________________

________________________________

________________________________

## I APPRECIATE MYSELF FOR

DID ANYTHING TRIGGER MY ANXIETY TODAY?

HOW DID I DEAL WITH IT?

HOW CAN I REFRAME MY ANXIOUS THOUGHTS TO FEEL BETTER?

THE BEST THING ABOUT TODAY

WHAT AM I EXCITED ABOUT FOR TOMORROW?

HOW WELL DID I MANAGE MY ANXIETY TODAY?

☆ ☆ ☆ ☆ ☆

# Wednesday

DATE: 

TODAY I FELT

## WHAT WAS ON MY MIND TODAY? HOW DID IT MAKE ME FEEL?

_______________________________________________

_______________________________________________

_______________________________________________

_______________________________________________

_______________________________________________

## WHAT WENT WELL TODAY?

_____________________________

_____________________________

_____________________________

_____________________________

_____________________________

_____________________________

_____________________________

_____________________________

_____________________________

## TODAY DID I...

○ SMILE

○ MEDITATE

○ EXERCISE

○ EAT NUTRITIOUS FOOD

○ CATCH FRESH AIR

○ SPEND TIME WITH THE PEOPLE I LOVE

○ SLEEP WELL

## THREE THINGS I AM GRATEFUL FOR

_____________________________

_____________________________

_____________________________

_____________________________

_____________________________

_____________________________

## I APPRECIATE MYSELF FOR

DID ANYTHING TRIGGER MY ANXIETY TODAY?

_______________________________________________

_______________________________________________

_______________________________________________

_______________________________________________

_______________________________________________

HOW DID I DEAL WITH IT?

_______________________________________________

_______________________________________________

_______________________________________________

_______________________________________________

_______________________________________________

HOW CAN I REFRAME MY ANXIOUS THOUGHTS TO FEEL BETTER?

_______________________________________________

_______________________________________________

_______________________________________________

_______________________________________________

_______________________________________________

THE BEST THING ABOUT TODAY

WHAT AM I EXCITED ABOUT FOR TOMORROW?

HOW WELL DID I MANAGE MY ANXIETY TODAY?

☆ ☆ ☆ ☆ ☆

# Thursday

DATE:

TODODAY I FELT

WHAT WAS ON MY MIND TODAY? HOW DID IT MAKE ME FEEL?

_______________________________________________

_______________________________________________

_______________________________________________

_______________________________________________

## WHAT WENT WELL TODAY?

_________________________________

_________________________________

_________________________________

_________________________________

_________________________________

_________________________________

_________________________________

_________________________________

_________________________________

## TODAY DID I...

- ○ SMILE
- ○ MEDITATE
- ○ EXERCISE
- ○ EAT NUTRITIOUS FOOD
- ○ CATCH FRESH AIR
- ○ SPEND TIME WITH THE PEOPLE I LOVE
- ○ SLEEP WELL

## THREE THINGS I AM GRATEFUL FOR

_________________________________

_________________________________

_________________________________

_________________________________

_________________________________

_________________________________

## I APPRECIATE MYSELF FOR

DID ANYTHING TRIGGER MY ANXIETY TODAY?

_______________________________________________

_______________________________________________

_______________________________________________

_______________________________________________

_______________________________________________

HOW DID I DEAL WITH IT?

_______________________________________________

_______________________________________________

_______________________________________________

_______________________________________________

_______________________________________________

HOW CAN I REFRAME MY ANXIOUS THOUGHTS TO FEEL BETTER?

_______________________________________________

_______________________________________________

_______________________________________________

_______________________________________________

_______________________________________________

THE BEST THING ABOUT TODAY

________________________________

________________________________

________________________________

________________________________

________________________________

________________________________

________________________________

WHAT AM I EXCITED ABOUT FOR TOMORROW?

HOW WELL DID I MANAGE MY ANXIETY TODAY?

☆ ☆ ☆ ☆ ☆

# *Friday*

DATE:

TODAY I FELT

## WHAT WAS ON MY MIND TODAY? HOW DID IT MAKE ME FEEL?

_______________________________________________

_______________________________________________

_______________________________________________

_______________________________________________

_______________________________________________

## WHAT WENT WELL TODAY?

_________________________________

_________________________________

_________________________________

_________________________________

_________________________________

_________________________________

_________________________________

_________________________________

_________________________________

## TODAY DID I...

○ SMILE

○ MEDITATE

○ EXERCISE

○ EAT NUTRITIOUS FOOD

○ CATCH FRESH AIR

○ SPEND TIME WITH THE
   PEOPLE I LOVE

○ SLEEP WELL

## THREE THINGS I AM GRATEFUL FOR

_________________________________

_________________________________

_________________________________

_________________________________

_________________________________

## I APPRECIATE MYSELF FOR

DID ANYTHING TRIGGER MY ANXIETY TODAY?

_______________________________________________

_______________________________________________

_______________________________________________

_______________________________________________

_______________________________________________

HOW DID I DEAL WITH IT?

_______________________________________________

_______________________________________________

_______________________________________________

_______________________________________________

_______________________________________________

HOW CAN I REFRAME MY ANXIOUS THOUGHTS TO FEEL BETTER?

_______________________________________________

_______________________________________________

_______________________________________________

_______________________________________________

_______________________________________________

THE BEST THING ABOUT TODAY

_______________________________

_______________________________

_______________________________

_______________________________

_______________________________

_______________________________

_______________________________

WHAT AM I EXCITED ABOUT FOR TOMORROW?

HOW WELL DID I MANAGE MY ANXIETY TODAY?

☆ ☆ ☆ ☆ ☆

# Saturday

DATE:

TODAY I FELT

_______________________________________________

**WHAT WAS ON MY MIND TODAY? HOW DID IT MAKE ME FEEL?**

_______________________________________________

_______________________________________________

_______________________________________________

_______________________________________________

_______________________________________________

**WHAT WENT WELL TODAY?**

_______________________________

_______________________________

_______________________________

_______________________________

_______________________________

_______________________________

_______________________________

**TODAY DID I...**

○ SMILE

○ MEDITATE

○ EXERCISE

○ EAT NUTRITIOUS FOOD

○ CATCH FRESH AIR

○ SPEND TIME WITH THE
PEOPLE I LOVE

○ SLEEP WELL

**THREE THINGS I AM GRATEFUL FOR**

_______________________________

_______________________________

_______________________________

_______________________________

_______________________________

**I APPRECIATE MYSELF FOR**

DID ANYTHING TRIGGER MY ANXIETY TODAY?

_______________________________________________

_______________________________________________

_______________________________________________

_______________________________________________

HOW DID I DEAL WITH IT?

_______________________________________________

_______________________________________________

_______________________________________________

_______________________________________________

HOW CAN I REFRAME MY ANXIOUS THOUGHTS TO FEEL BETTER?

_______________________________________________

_______________________________________________

_______________________________________________

_______________________________________________

THE BEST THING ABOUT TODAY

___________________________

___________________________

___________________________

___________________________

___________________________

___________________________

WHAT AM I EXCITED ABOUT FOR TOMORROW?

HOW WELL DID I MANAGE MY ANXIETY TODAY?

☆ ☆ ☆ ☆ ☆

# Sunday

DATE:

TODAY I FELT

## WHAT WAS ON MY MIND TODAY? HOW DID IT MAKE ME FEEL?

_______________________________________________

_______________________________________________

_______________________________________________

_______________________________________________

## WHAT WENT WELL TODAY?

_____________________________

_____________________________

_____________________________

_____________________________

_____________________________

_____________________________

_____________________________

## TODAY DID I...

○ SMILE

○ MEDITATE

○ EXERCISE

○ EAT NUTRITIOUS FOOD

○ CATCH FRESH AIR

○ SPEND TIME WITH THE
PEOPLE I LOVE

○ SLEEP WELL

## THREE THINGS I AM GRATEFUL FOR

_____________________________

_____________________________

_____________________________

_____________________________

_____________________________

## I APPRECIATE MYSELF FOR

DID ANYTHING TRIGGER MY ANXIETY TODAY?

HOW DID I DEAL WITH IT?

HOW CAN I REFRAME MY ANXIOUS THOUGHTS TO FEEL BETTER?

THE BEST THING ABOUT TODAY

WHAT AM I EXCITED ABOUT FOR TOMORROW?

HOW WELL DID I MANAGE MY ANXIETY TODAY?

☆ ☆ ☆ ☆ ☆

# Week 11
## Check in

WHAT DID I DO WELL THIS WEEK?

______________________________________________

______________________________________________

______________________________________________

______________________________________________

THIS WEEK I FELT

HOW WELL DID I MANAGE MY ANXIETY THIS WEEK?

WHAT DID I DO WELL THIS WEEK?

______________________________________________

______________________________________________

______________________________________________

______________________________________________

WHAT WOULD I LIKE TO DO BETTER NEXT WEEK?

WHAT AM I EXCITED ABOUT IN THE UPCOMING WEEK?

# Reflecting on Your 12-week Journey

> WE ALL MAKE MISTAKES, HAVE STRUGGLES, AND EVEN REGRET THINGS IN OUR PAST. BUT YOU ARE NOT YOUR MISTAKES OR YOUR STRUGGLES. YOU ARE HERE NOW WITH THE POWER TO SHAPE YOUR DAY AND YOUR FUTURE.
>
> – STEVE MARABOLI

# Reflecting on Your 12-week Journey

We have now come to the end of a 12-week-long journey. Let us take a moment to reflect on how our journaling efforts have rewarded us—what we have learned and what we intend to pursue in the future.

How was your physical and emotional health before you started journaling?

___________________________________________

___________________________________________

___________________________________________

How is your physical and emotional health after journaling for 12 weeks?

___________________________________________

___________________________________________

___________________________________________

Has your anxiety reduced over the course of these 12 weeks of journaling?

___________________________________________

___________________________________________

___________________________________________

Identify three changes to your mindset, behavior, or overall well-being.

___________________________________________

___________________________________________

___________________________________________

Did you journal as regularly as you would have liked to? If not, what could help you improve your consistency going forward?

___________________________________________

___________________________________________

___________________________________________

Do you want to continue your journaling practice?

___________________________________________

What simple steps can you take right away to continue journaling?

___________________________________________

___________________________________________

Which specific sections of this book helped you
the most?

_______________________________________________

_______________________________________________

_______________________________________________

How will you continue to incorporate them into
your daily life?

_______________________________________________

_______________________________________________

_______________________________________________

Any Closing Thoughts?

_______________________________________________

_______________________________________________

_______________________________________________

_______________________________________________

_______________________________________________

# Monday

DATE:

TODAY I FELT

WHAT WAS ON MY MIND TODAY? HOW DID IT MAKE ME FEEL?

_______________________________________________

_______________________________________________

_______________________________________________

_______________________________________________

WHAT WENT WELL TODAY?

TODAY DID I...

○ SMILE

○ MEDITATE

○ EXERCISE

○ EAT NUTRITIOUS FOOD

○ CATCH FRESH AIR

○ SPEND TIME WITH THE
PEOPLE I LOVE

○ SLEEP WELL

THREE THINGS I AM GRATEFUL FOR

I APPRECIATE MYSELF FOR

DID ANYTHING TRIGGER MY ANXIETY TODAY?

HOW DID I DEAL WITH IT?

HOW CAN I REFRAME MY ANXIOUS THOUGHTS TO FEEL BETTER?

THE BEST THING ABOUT TODAY

WHAT AM I EXCITED ABOUT FOR TOMORROW?

HOW WELL DID I MANAGE MY ANXIETY TODAY?

# Tuesday

DATE:

TODAY I FELT
_________________________________

## WHAT WAS ON MY MIND TODAY? HOW DID IT MAKE ME FEEL?

_______________________________________________

_______________________________________________

_______________________________________________

_______________________________________________

## WHAT WENT WELL TODAY?

____________________________

____________________________

____________________________

____________________________

____________________________

____________________________

____________________________

____________________________

## TODAY DID I...

○ SMILE

○ MEDITATE

○ EXERCISE

○ EAT NUTRITIOUS FOOD

○ CATCH FRESH AIR

○ SPEND TIME WITH THE
  PEOPLE I LOVE

○ SLEEP WELL

## THREE THINGS I AM GRATEFUL FOR

____________________________

____________________________

____________________________

____________________________

## I APPRECIATE MYSELF FOR

DID ANYTHING TRIGGER MY ANXIETY TODAY?

_______________________________________________

_______________________________________________

_______________________________________________

_______________________________________________

_______________________________________________

HOW DID I DEAL WITH IT?

_______________________________________________

_______________________________________________

_______________________________________________

_______________________________________________

_______________________________________________

HOW CAN I REFRAME MY ANXIOUS THOUGHTS TO FEEL BETTER?

_______________________________________________

_______________________________________________

_______________________________________________

_______________________________________________

_______________________________________________

THE BEST THING ABOUT TODAY

_________________________________

_________________________________

_________________________________

_________________________________

_________________________________

_________________________________

WHAT AM I EXCITED ABOUT FOR TOMORROW?

HOW WELL DID I MANAGE MY ANXIETY TODAY?

☆ ☆ ☆ ☆ ☆

# Wednesday

DATE:

TODAY I FELT

## WHAT WAS ON MY MIND TODAY? HOW DID IT MAKE ME FEEL?

____________________________________________

____________________________________________

____________________________________________

____________________________________________

## WHAT WENT WELL TODAY?

________________________________

________________________________

________________________________

________________________________

________________________________

________________________________

________________________________

________________________________

## TODAY DID I...

○ SMILE

○ MEDITATE

○ EXERCISE

○ EAT NUTRITIOUS FOOD

○ CATCH FRESH AIR

○ SPEND TIME WITH THE PEOPLE I LOVE

○ SLEEP WELL

## THREE THINGS I AM GRATEFUL FOR

________________________________

________________________________

________________________________

________________________________

________________________________

## I APPRECIATE MYSELF FOR

DID ANYTHING TRIGGER MY ANXIETY TODAY?

HOW DID I DEAL WITH IT?

HOW CAN I REFRAME MY ANXIOUS THOUGHTS TO FEEL BETTER?

THE BEST THING ABOUT TODAY

WHAT AM I EXCITED ABOUT FOR TOMORROW?

HOW WELL DID I MANAGE MY ANXIETY TODAY?

☆ ☆ ☆ ☆ ☆

# Thursday

DATE:

TODAY I FELT
_______________________________

## WHAT WAS ON MY MIND TODAY? HOW DID IT MAKE ME FEEL?

_________________________________________

_________________________________________

_________________________________________

_________________________________________

## WHAT WENT WELL TODAY?

______________________________

______________________________

______________________________

______________________________

______________________________

______________________________

______________________________

______________________________

## TODAY DID I...

- ○ SMILE
- ○ MEDITATE
- ○ EXERCISE
- ○ EAT NUTRITIOUS FOOD
- ○ CATCH FRESH AIR
- ○ SPEND TIME WITH THE PEOPLE I LOVE
- ○ SLEEP WELL

## THREE THINGS I AM GRATEFUL FOR

______________________________

______________________________

______________________________

______________________________

______________________________

## I APPRECIATE MYSELF FOR

DID ANYTHING TRIGGER MY ANXIETY TODAY?

HOW DID I DEAL WITH IT?

HOW CAN I REFRAME MY ANXIOUS THOUGHTS TO FEEL BETTER?

THE BEST THING ABOUT TODAY

WHAT AM I EXCITED ABOUT FOR TOMORROW?

HOW WELL DID I MANAGE MY ANXIETY TODAY?

☆ ☆ ☆ ☆ ☆

# Friday

DATE:

TODAY I FELT

## WHAT WAS ON MY MIND TODAY? HOW DID IT MAKE ME FEEL?

_______________________________________________

_______________________________________________

_______________________________________________

_______________________________________________

## WHAT WENT WELL TODAY?

_________________________________

_________________________________

_________________________________

_________________________________

_________________________________

_________________________________

_________________________________

_________________________________

## TODAY DID I...

- ○ SMILE
- ○ MEDITATE
- ○ EXERCISE
- ○ EAT NUTRITIOUS FOOD
- ○ CATCH FRESH AIR
- ○ SPEND TIME WITH THE PEOPLE I LOVE
- ○ SLEEP WELL

## THREE THINGS I AM GRATEFUL FOR

_________________________________

_________________________________

_________________________________

_________________________________

_________________________________

_________________________________

## I APPRECIATE MYSELF FOR

DID ANYTHING TRIGGER MY ANXIETY TODAY?

___________________________________________

___________________________________________

___________________________________________

___________________________________________

HOW DID I DEAL WITH IT?

___________________________________________

___________________________________________

___________________________________________

___________________________________________

HOW CAN I REFRAME MY ANXIOUS THOUGHTS TO FEEL BETTER?

___________________________________________

___________________________________________

___________________________________________

___________________________________________

THE BEST THING ABOUT TODAY

_____________________________

_____________________________

_____________________________

_____________________________

_____________________________

_____________________________

WHAT AM I EXCITED ABOUT FOR TOMORROW?




HOW WELL DID I MANAGE MY ANXIETY TODAY?

☆ ☆ ☆ ☆ ☆

# Saturday

## WHAT WAS ON MY MIND TODAY? HOW DID IT MAKE ME FEEL?

_______________________________________________

_______________________________________________

_______________________________________________

_______________________________________________

## WHAT WENT WELL TODAY?

________________________________

________________________________

________________________________

________________________________

________________________________

________________________________

________________________________

________________________________

## TODAY DID I...

○ SMILE

○ MEDITATE

○ EXERCISE

○ EAT NUTRITIOUS FOOD

○ CATCH FRESH AIR

○ SPEND TIME WITH THE PEOPLE I LOVE

○ SLEEP WELL

## THREE THINGS I AM GRATEFUL FOR

________________________________

________________________________

________________________________

________________________________

________________________________

## I APPRECIATE MYSELF FOR

DID ANYTHING TRIGGER MY ANXIETY TODAY?

HOW DID I DEAL WITH IT?

HOW CAN I REFRAME MY ANXIOUS THOUGHTS TO FEEL BETTER?

THE BEST THING ABOUT TODAY

WHAT AM I EXCITED ABOUT FOR TOMORROW?

HOW WELL DID I MANAGE MY ANXIETY TODAY?

☆ ☆ ☆ ☆ ☆

# Sunday

DATE:

TODAY I FELT

WHAT WAS ON MY MIND TODAY? HOW DID IT MAKE ME FEEL?

______________________________________________

______________________________________________

______________________________________________

______________________________________________

______________________________________________

WHAT WENT WELL TODAY?

___________________________________

___________________________________

___________________________________

___________________________________

___________________________________

___________________________________

___________________________________

___________________________________

TODAY DID I...

○ SMILE

○ MEDITATE

○ EXERCISE

○ EAT NUTRITIOUS FOOD

○ CATCH FRESH AIR

○ SPEND TIME WITH THE PEOPLE I LOVE

○ SLEEP WELL

THREE THINGS I AM GRATEFUL FOR

___________________________________

___________________________________

___________________________________

___________________________________

___________________________________

I APPRECIATE MYSELF FOR

DID ANYTHING TRIGGER MY ANXIETY TODAY?

HOW DID I DEAL WITH IT?

HOW CAN I REFRAME MY ANXIOUS THOUGHTS TO FEEL BETTER?

THE BEST THING ABOUT TODAY

WHAT AM I EXCITED ABOUT FOR TOMORROW?

HOW WELL DID I MANAGE MY ANXIETY TODAY?

☆ ☆ ☆ ☆ ☆

# Week 12
## Check in

DATE:

**WHAT DID I DO WELL THIS WEEK?**

_______________________________________

_______________________________________

_______________________________________

_______________________________________

**THIS WEEK I FELT**

**HOW WELL DID I MANAGE MY ANXIETY THIS WEEK?**

☆ ☆ ☆ ☆ ☆

**WHAT DID I DO WELL THIS WEEK?**

_______________________________________

_______________________________________

_______________________________________

_______________________________________

**WHAT WOULD I LIKE TO DO BETTER NEXT WEEK?**

**WHAT AM I EXCITED ABOUT IN THE UPCOMING WEEK?**

# Month 3
## Check in

HOW WELL DID I MANAGE MY ANXIETY THIS MONTH?

HOW DO I FEEL ABOUT THIS MONTH?

_________________________________________________

_________________________________________________

_________________________________________________

MY ACCOMPLISHMENTS THIS MONTH

1          2          3

WHAT HELPED ME STAY CALM THIS MONTH?

_________________________________________________

_________________________________________________

_________________________________________________

_________________________________________________

HOW HAVE I GROWN THIS MONTH?

________________________

________________________

________________________

________________________

________________________

WHAT DO I WANT TO DO DIFFERENTLY NEXT MONTH?

________________________

________________________

________________________

________________________

________________________

# Let's Color

# Reflections

*Do you want to continue journaling?*

Log on to Amazon and buy another copy of this journal today!

*Your free Journal*

Subscribe to my newsletter
& grab your FREE copy of
the 'Being Yourself Journal'
today!
Log on to romasharma.com

*For more of my books*

**Log on to romasharma.com**